Bar and Club Design
Bethan Ryder

First published in the United States of America in 2002
by Abbeville Press
116 West 23rd Street
New York, NY 10011

First published in Great Britain in 2002
by Laurence King Publishing
71 Great Russell Street
London WC1B 3BP

Printed in Hong Kong

First Edition

ISBN 0-7892-0819-9

10   9   8   7   6   5   4   3   2   1

Library of Congress Cataloging-in-Publication Data
Ryder, Bethan.
     Bar and club design/ Bethan Ryder.
         p. cm.
     Includes index.
     ISBN 0-7892-0819-9 (alk. paper)
     1. Bars (Drinking establishments) 2. Interior decoration—
History—20th century. 3. Interior architecture—History—
20th century. I. Title

NK2195.R4 R93 2002
747—dc21
                                        2001053562

Design: Blast
Divider photography: Rob Lawson

Abbeville Press Publishers
New York London

Bar and Club Design
Bethan Ryder

Contents

84 Hotel bars 124 Clubs 188 Index and credits

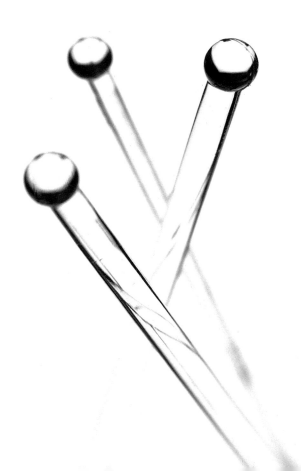

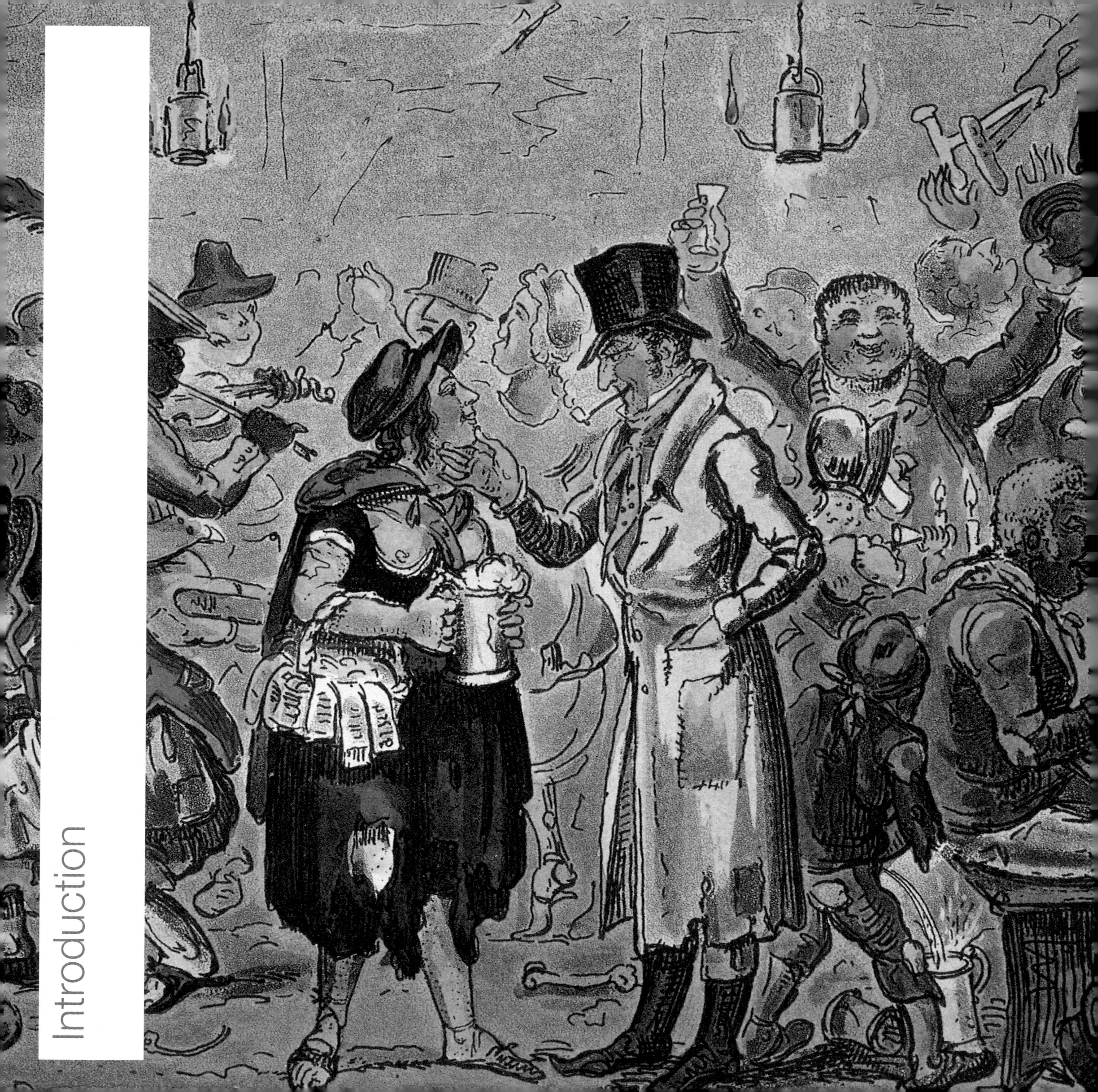

Introduction

Bawdy times: All walks of London life live it up in an early 19th-century tavern.

20 years ago, a book on bar and club design would not have been possible. There simply weren't enough venues to warrant such a particular survey. At the turn of the new millennium, every city in the developed world has more than enough bars and clubs to call their own. The projects featured in this book are only a small selection, chosen for their innovative design, uniqueness or sheer beauty. They are very much considered, 'styled' spaces, rather than simply functional places in which to drink or dance. Most of the projects were completed over the past two years, so, as a whole, they capture the design Zeitgeist of international venues where night becomes play.

Bars and clubs can be located within the wider context of commercial leisure spaces. Hotels, restaurants, bars and clubs all originate from the inn or tavern of the 17th century and, centuries later, they remain public arenas where people socialize and interact. In the late 20th century, we witnessed an increase in both the volume and diversity of leisure spaces in the 'developed world'; the restaurant business is booming, café chains thriving, 'boutique' hotels flourishing, with traditional chain hotels also expanding. As travel, technology, media and telecommunications continue to shrink the globe, the inhabitants of the Western World increasingly live by the screen and the magazine – lifestyle is all.

These public, commercial spaces are where the modern urbanite 'performs' her or his identity – where you eat, drink and sleep defines, to a large extent, your social self.

As technological developments, such as the internet, render (to a certain degree) traditional public institutions, such as banks, shops and offices, obsolete, there is perhaps an even greater need for social arenas where individuals of the e-mail and dot.com age can actually interact and communicate with others on a basic human level. Maybe life's mundane tasks can be taken care of by new technology, but meeting people on-line will never quite usurp genuine human contact.

The modern professional is no longer required to work in a fixed place – laptops and mobile phones allow a mobility and flexibility unimaginable in previous decades. In the same way that travel and greater social movement in the 17th and 18th centuries led to creation of the public house, inn and tavern in Britain and the New World, places that provided refreshment and respite for travellers, so they remain a necessity today. The resurgence of cocktail culture and the increase in the sheer volume of cafés, restaurants, lounges and hotel lobbies can also be viewed as something of a fin-de-siècle, cyclical repetition of the grand saloon days of the late 19th century, an idea to which I shall return later.

A survey of bar and club design would not be valid without an examination of the recent developments in restaurant and hotel design. Likewise, underground club culture as a more anarchic influence is worthy of attention in terms of developments in nightclub design. For the purposes of structure, this book is divided into three

Cocktail hour in the Rubber Room – a 1930s hotel bar in Ohio, USA, which was almost entirely constructed of rubber.

parts – bars & restaurant bars, hotel bars, and nightclubs. These categories serve merely a functional purpose, allowing readers easy navigation in their search for a particular type of bar or club. The groupings are not rigid or definitive – as you will see in the course of this book, it is in some senses impossible to make such distinctions, as boundaries between different types of drinking or nocturnal establishment have become blurred. Moreover, within each category there is enormous diversity.

The word 'bar' has come to mean so much more than its original and most simplistic definition: 'A straight piece of wood, metal, or other rigid material, long in proportion to its thickness' (Oxford English Dictionary). This, of course, is what most bars contain – a counter over which alcoholic and/or other refreshments are served by a bartender. But the word has come to signify 'the room or premises containing such a counter' and it is the design of this kind of bar that is the focus of this book.

It is worth, at this point, noting the distinction between pub (public house) and bar. The projects in this book are places where, one might argue, style takes precedence over function. They are modern, spectacular forums, underpinned by the ideas of display and performance, rather than utilitarian, more casual places in which people meet, drink and gossip – such as the pub. Although Britain, in the past, had plenty of taverns and inns, to understand the concept of the 'bar' in the context of this book we must look to America. Even British gin palaces

were about selling a product, more often than not to the lower classes, rather than providing a glamorous arena for the display of riches. According to Andrew Barr (*Drink: A Social History of America*, Pimlico, London, 1995), before the 19th century, British public houses could only be distinguished from private houses by a sign on the door. Once inside, they were divided 'into tap room, public parlour, bar, kitchen and publican's private parlour'. The design was basic and functional; only parlours, occasionally, had proper tables and chairs, as opposed to wooden benches. The retail revolution of the 1820s steered pub design towards that of the dram shop, which had emerged in response to the popularity of gin, leading to the introduction of a 'bar' into the public house. The inventions of gas lighting and plate glass meant that 'the gin palaces of the 1830s were simply glamorous-looking shops from which customers bought alcoholic drinks to take away or to drink standing up on the premises.' While perpendicular drinking increased sales, it was also bound up with class. The lower classes drank publicly at the bar, while the better-bred imbibed in the comfort of their own homes.

No, for the recent cocktail revival worldwide and the sophisticated drinking establishments that emerged in the latter part of the 20th century, and which we have come to expect in every modern city, we are indebted to the land of dreams, excess, entertainment and conspicuous consumption – the US. It is no coincidence that where there are riches, there are bars, and, at the end of the

19th century, the 'brave new world' was the wealthiest place to be.

William Grimes examines the reason why the US is so representative of bar and cocktail culture in his book *Straight Up or On the Rocks: A Cultural History of American Drink* (Simon & Schuster, 1993). He believes the reasons can be found at the very roots of American society: 'The colonists chose to breathe a freer, harsher air. Along with the constraints that made the villages and towns of the Old World deadly and claustrophobic, they threw off the warm blanket of custom, family ties, friendships and loyalties. Competitive and mobile, Americans had to develop social forms that promote quick and effortless acquaintance rather than strong lasting ties.' He goes on to argue that the cocktail, as a mixture of sometimes wildly different ingredients, is itself symbolic of the cultural melting pot of American society and of a break with the pre-industrial past.

It is fascinating to compare today's drinking scene with the American saloons of the 19th-century gold rush era that Grimes describes, when champagne flowed through cities 'like a mighty, coursing river'. 'It was the age of "more is more", and not only in decoration. America took an uncomplicated attitude towards wealth and display.... The oxymoronic notion of intimate public space did not exist. Life outside the home was lived on a theatrical, heroic scale.' This was a time when there were millionaires and the rich wanted to celebrate their lavish lifestyles in

Speakeasies were the secret drinking dens and clubs of the US during the Prohibition era of the 1920s.

public, a desire which informed the growth of bars and restaurants. The design of such places at this time tended to be heavy, ornate and Victorian, as Grimes, quoting Henry L Mencken, points out: 'Saloon architects stuck to mirrors as God first made them, to honest brass, and to noble and imperishable mahogany.' Grimes goes on to write that, 'Rare was the establishment that did not advertise its "mile-long bar".' Sounds familiar? Recently, the press releases of many new bars around the globe have boasted that they have the longest bar in London, Europe, etc.

Although parallels can be drawn between the current explosion of new bars at the turn of the 21st century and the grand saloons of late 19th-century America, it should be noted that many of today's venues are very much bound up with the recent 'restaurant revolution'. World cities, such as Los Angeles, New York, London and Sydney, have seen a huge increase in the amount and diversity of restaurants over the past 20 years, and this has led to bar design receiving a more privileged status. Much of this has occurred as a result of increased international travel and the fact that people are now able to experience many different cultures. London entrepreneurs, such as Sir Terence Conran (Quaglino's, Mezzo, Sartoria and many more) and Oliver Peyton (Atlantic Bar & Grill, Mash), and New York's Keith McNally (Balthazar and Pasteis) are recognized as incredibly influential in terms of creating the 'designer' restaurant industry and, subsequently, the bar scene, which in

turn has been copied the world over. Yet these pioneers were themselves influenced originally by French and Italian gastronomy.

The emergence of a dynamic restaurant and bar industry happened after the 1980s, a period, at least in Manhattan and London, of conspicuous riches and excess. The abundance of wealth created a demand for social stages where the media creative or businessman could do their deals, or simply live it up in the company of other equally style conscious or moneyed citizens. Designer restaurants and bars across the world form a kind of a club for jet-setters and those involved in the image industries. In Manhattan, it is common for many top restaurants to provide a bar for non-dining patrons. Obviously, this increases the profit for the owner, but also allows those keen to be seen in the right places the opportunity, at least, to sip a Martini at, for example, Balthazar or the Seagram Brasserie (see page 68), without having to attempt the impossible and gain a reservation. Such a layout increases the venue's popularity and 'buzz' – some restaurants' bars are created as part of the main dining room, whereas others are separate, yet connected spaces, such as Shu (see page 32).

Hotels and their bars are 'hip' again, as they were in the latter part of the 19th century. Lucius Beebe, author of *The Stork Club Bar Book* (J J Little & Ives Company, New York, 1946), reminds us that 'the history of Greece is written in its temples, that of the United States in its

The freaks come out at night at probably the world's most famous disco – Manhattan's Studio 54.

hotels'. He continues: 'To carry the parallel even farther, a good deal of the history of New York has been written in its restaurants, saloons, night clubs, cafés, cabarets, bars, lounges, dining rooms, ordinaires, fish and chip shops, chophouses, dives, deadfalls, beer stubes, dramshops and the allied institutions dedicated to the stoking and sluicing of customers of many tastes and means.' It is Grimes again who reminds us how the hotel bar was used at that time, describing them as the finest semi-public institutions: 'Non-guests felt free to stroll into a fine hotel lobby, settle down in a comfortable chair and read a newspaper, write a letter or two on the house stationery.' He refers to Hoffman House as New York's most salubrious venue, with apparently no less than 17 bartenders and a large number of huge mirrors. These hotel saloons, the 'glittering stage for the grand gesture', were eventually ruined by Prohibition in the 1920s.

The renaissance of today's hotel bars can be accredited to two men – Ian Schrager and designer Philippe Starck. Between them they have not only created 'destination hotels' – places that are worth a trip in themselves – but also bars that are utilized both by the cosmopolitan, style-conscious hotel guests and the 'local' movers and shakers of the city. Philippe Starck designed the Oyster Bar in the Peninsula Hotel's Felix Restaurant in Hong Kong (1994) and also Café Costes in Paris (1984), spaces so theatrical and glamorous they attracted both international guests and the city's finest. It was Ian Schrager, the man behind the legendary 1970s nightclub Studio 54, who

coined the phrase 'lobby living' and declared that he would make hotels the nightclubs of the 1990s. Looking at hotel bars as diverse as the Met Bar (one of London's first 'independent' hotel bars) and Atoll, Heligoland (see page 106), and the Hudson in New York (see page 114), Schrager seems to have succeeded.

A trend in hotel bar design has been to create a separate entrance to the one from the lobby – London-based design practice United Designers modelled the Met Bar, at least in theory, on Schrager's glamorous, star-studded Manhattan hotel bars, such as the Royalton and Paramount. They ensured a certain cachet for those dwelling in the city by forming a street entrance, making the bar 'members only', except for hotel residents. Now that design is a huge influence in the hotel market, many hoteliers are paying considerable attention to their bars, realizing the extent of the revenue to be made from creating something more than simply a resting place for guests. Independent hoteliers have followed this trend, from Andre Balazs's Mercer (by Christian Liagre), which contains a French café-style bar, to the Morrison in Dublin (design concept by John Rocha), which has three popular bars. An example of a large corporate chain is Starwood's 'W' hotel chain, with their hip Whisky Bars. Even classic hotels, such as London's Claridge's (see page 90) and the Berkeley, are adding new bars, both by David Collins, albeit in a way that is fairly traditional and sensitive to the existing architecture.

Hotel bars in the 21st century can range from quiet, relaxing and comfortable lounges, such as Bar Tempo in Japan (see page 86), to bright, loud and buzzing showcases, like the Long Bar at the Sanderson Hotel in London, and to late-night DJ bars, like the Met Bar or Time (Intergalactic) Beach Bar in Whitley Bay, UK (see page 98). Basically, anything goes.

It is difficult to trace the true origins of the nightclub – to a certain extent, they have always been whatever a bar or pub is not, i.e. a place to visit after hours, sometimes illegal, to continue drinking and dancing. Sheryl Garratt, in her informative book on club culture *Adventures in Wonderland: A Decade of Club Culture* (Headline, London, 1999), describes how nightclubs originated from the subversive roots of disco and the 'discothèque', citing Albert Goldman in his book *Disco*: 'The first place of public entertainment to use the word was a bar in the rue Huchette in Paris before the Second World War.' As she explains, these venues at that time were makeshift underground clubs, where people danced to jazz and American swing music.

Since club culture has often operated on the margins (a new youth trend usually starts 'undergound', before it is assimilated into the mainstream and commodified), perhaps, as Grimes argues, the speakeasy of the Prohibition era might be identified as being at the roots of today's nightclub. (Speakeasies were secret adult playgrounds, in the same way that many clubs today

have an entry policy or membership card – look right and you can come in, just like knowing the correct password in the 1920s.) In fact, places like the Stork Club in New York did indeed make the transition from speakeasy to legal nightspot, and the nightclubs of the 1940s, such as the star-studded Hollywood supper club-style clubs, like Ciro's and the Mocambo on Sunset Strip, were natural descendants of the speakeasy. It is interesting to note that, as soon as women began to drink alongside men, the interiors and decor of night-time venues became more considered.

When you read stories of the decadent, glamorous (and illegal) goings-on in the speakeasy, designed to fly in the face of the authorities, it almost puts the organized, large-budget production dance raves of the mid-1990s to shame. Of one in particular, Suzanne Matczuk writes, 'There was the Merry-Go-Round, an elaborate set-up with carousel horses for bar stools and a rotating bar. Sharp dressed guys and ultra-chic gals perched on ponies sipping clover clubs and champagne cocktails – going around and around every eleven minutes to the surreal sounds of the electric organ' (*Cocktail-O-Matic: The Little Black Book of Cocktails*, Bain & Cox, 1998).

Grimes's descriptions too make the speakeasy appear to be the ancestor of the parties of the 1990s (where drugs, instead of alcohol, are the illegal substance being consumed). 'A top-of-the-line speak might boast two bars, a dance floor, Ping Pong and backgammon rooms,

lounges, an art gallery and a band.' Just substitute video projections for art gallery and DJs for the band and you have something similar to clubs at the end of the 20th century. Other speakeasies appear to have been as refined as modern hotel bars: 'The Park Avenue Club in New York, designed by Joseph Urban, had an octagonal bar surrounded by floor-to-ceiling mirrors.' (Think of the octagonal bar in Dublin's Clarence Hotel and it is easy to argue that things haven't changed.) Such styled interiors were all about tempting the wealthy gentlemen and ladies to live it up in secret, glamorous surroundings.

Back then, live music and cabaret were the entertainment. Dance halls and ballrooms were created, with large bands playing for dancing couples. It wasn't really until the 1960s that vinyl introduced the DJ, and dance clubs that are comparable with the modern nightclub really began to emerge. As Sheryl Garratt writes, 'After the war, Paul Racine continued the trend of dancing to records rather than live music with his Whiskey à Go-Go clubs.' The first opened in Paris in 1947, with a similar club opening on Sunset Strip in LA. Garratt describes the decor of two UK discos of the early 1960s: 'La Discothèque on Wardour Street tuned into the new sexual freedoms, with double beds on and around the dance floor. In 1962, the Place opened up in Hanley, near Stoke-on-Trent, with red lighting and all-black decor, except for a gold-painted entrance hall, mock leopardskin wallpaper in the toilets and a small sitting room called the Fridge that was all-white with blue lighting – the first chill-out rooms perhaps.'

Garratt claims that it was in New York that the discothèque became 'disco': 'The first establishment to open in New York was modelled on the French clubs and intended exclusively for the rich and famous.' Of course, the decade that saw the glitterball of disco truly spin was the 1970s, when many venues were created in disused theatres and dancehalls, as a hedonistic escape from daily life. In fact, the *Daily News* in New York reported that the city had been 'Swept away on a Wild Wave of Disco-mania' (see *Contract Interiors*, November 1977). The most legendary place by far was Studio 54, Ian Schrager and his late partner Steve Rubell's brief, but immortal, disco, opening in 1977 in an old opera house dating back to 1927 (but which had been, more recently, occupied by CBS – hence the name *Studio* 54). According to *Contract Interiors*, Ron Doud's design respected the original interior: 'The elaborate neo-classical moldings and plasterwork simply cleaned and highlighted with glossy paint and careful lighting.' Furnishings were flexible and included 'ten eight-foot-square modular seating units covered in silver vinyl'.

Studio 54 had many of the characteristics that exist in modern nightclubs – spectacular lighting and hundreds of visual effects, plus a 'theatrical' layout. The spectacle was ensured by the physical structure of the space – the balcony and stage were still in place. The balcony, with its seating and tables, hung above the large parquet dance floor. Silver banquettes surrounded the dance floor and there was a mirrored, diamond-shaped bar. The VIP room was in the basement. Studio 54's life span was only 33 months, although the memory of it still sparkles on.

In her book, Sheryl Garratt charts the birth of seminal Manhattan and Chicago clubs in the cities' gay venues, such as the Paradise Garage and the Loft. Although these clubs were vital in the development of clubs today, such as New York's Twilos and London's Ministry of Sound and Fabric, the forerunners were almost anti-designed. Paradise Garage was housed in a former cast-concrete parking garage, where the all-important feature was the sound system by sound innovator Richard Long (who later designed the Ministry of Sound's system). Likewise, places such as the Tunnel in New York, created in the late 1980s, were constructed in former industrial buildings, like power stations and ex-warehouses. Some argue that this is the etymology of the term 'house' music.

Designer Ben Kelly's Haçienda in Manchester, and the Ministry of Sound designed by Lynn Davies, were influenced by this industrial, warehouse look. As Garratt recalls of the Haçienda, 'There were no sticky carpets. No mirrorballs and dark recesses. Light and spacious, with a high roof, bare brick walls, pillars painted in hazard stripes and traffic bollards round the outside of the dance floor, it was as far from the traditional British nightclub as could be conceived.' Located in an ex-yacht warehouse, the interior was directly inspired by the owners' (band New Order) visits to places like Danceteria in New York. It opened in 1982, although its heyday was the 'summer

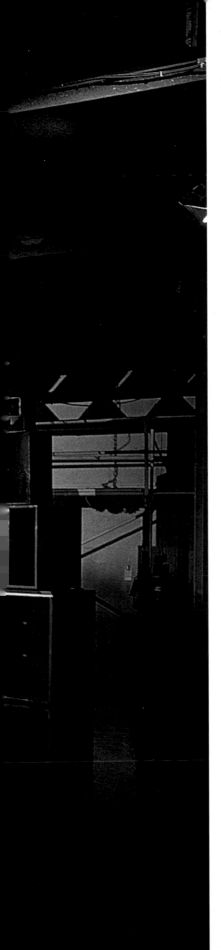

of love' of 1988. Fairly soon, exposed brick ceilings, a maze of silver spaghetti-like ducts and a simple, bare box for dancing became the nightclub design norm. Despite the introduction of more comfortable chill-out lounge areas, in the late 1980s and early 1990s, all anyone cared about was the music (thanks to the popularity of the drug ecstasy), spending most of their time dancing euphorically.

In 2001 there is still a clear demand for dance clubs, as the creation of London's The End and Fabric demonstrate. Both have raw, basic industrial interiors and place great emphasis on technology, incorporating state-of-the-art visuals, lighting and impressive digital communication systems. Fabric, for example, boasts a 'Body Sonic' dance floor that vibrates with the music. But the clubbing generation that were once quite happy to dance in sweaty music boxes have grown up and now want something more sophisticated. Hence the revival of cocktail culture by and for the PEPSI (post-ecstasy, pre-senility) generation, and the growth of late-night bar-cum-clubs that play more leisurely, or at least muted, beats than Balearic, but still recognize the importance of the DJ.

Nowadays, the lounge/chill-out area is likely to be larger than the dance floor – examples include Chinawhite (see page 142), NASA (see page 182) and Lux (see page 164). Even a venue like B 018 (see page 126) has dancing platforms that transform into sofas and chairs. There will always be venues dedicated to dancing, such as the Bomb (see page 134) or Next (see page 140), but

increasingly operators are allowing dancing throughout their venue, or setting aside a small space specifically for it. If speed and ecstasy were once the drugs of choice, fuelling acid house and raves, the favoured recreational drug for the older, ex-clubbing generation is more likely to be cocaine. Who needs frantic dancing when such a drug is so suited to lounging about and chatting?

Yet cocktail culture, in louche, designer surroundings, has, to an extent, usurped these dance clubs, and 'cocktail lounges', such as the 10 Room chain in London, and New York venues like Lot 61, Joe's Pub, Moomba and the Lotus Rooms, are the places to see and be seen. Not to mention hotel bars, some of which have become modern-day nightclubs, such as the Hudson with its Saturday-Night-Fever floor. Escapism is nowadays less about getting lost in music on the packed dance floor, and more about glamour and gloss. But bar and club design is a very ephemeral thing – today's hot spots can very soon be left out in the cold. Next year's trend could be the antithesis of current fashions.

Flexible Times

The burgeoning leisure and travel market and the increase in commercial venues catering for recreation and business, have made operators realize that today's discerning consumer wants choice. In response to this, operators attempt to maximize their profits and improve the longevity of their businesses by ensuring that their venue has broad appeal and has a variety of functions.

As city dwellers, inhabiting small living spaces, increasingly pursue a consciously considered 'lifestyle' that involves eating and drinking outside the home, bar owners and restaurateurs are seeking to satisfy the well-travelled, sophisticated customer.

Architects and designers are being asked to create interiors that can operate as both day and night venues, whether they be café-bars that become night-time lounges or multipurpose venues that offer drinking, dining and dancing all under one roof. In some ways, this is no different to the speakeasy of the Prohibition era in the US, which evolved into the nightclubs and dance halls of the 1940s and 1950s.

New technology has played an important part in creating this flexibility within modern bar design. Lighting and film effects have been tried and tested in clubs, often minimal or even 'anti-design' places. Their bare walls provide a good blank canvas for projections. Such effects are now being introduced into bars. There is no doubt that many of the late-night cocktail and lounge venues have been created by, and for, the ex-clubbing generation. The thirtysomething professionals of the world's developed cities, who once went clubbing regularly and were part of the ecstasy culture, attending illegal parties and frequenting rough-and-ready venues, have helped to develop and appreciated a more sophisticated bar scene.

A good example of flexibility through design, or perhaps decoration, are clubs like London's Raw, which used to change their interiors annually. This is where the restaurateur-entrepreneur Oliver Peyton began, going on to become the owner of the seminal Atlantic Bar & Grill in London and the Mash restaurants and bars.

So, there are two strands to 'flexible spaces' – the multipurpose venues that accommodate several purposes and those that appear to have assimilated new technology in order to change the interior. Examples of the former include restaurant bars with a separate, distinct space, such as Shu, or even the Church Lounge (see page 122), Embassy (see page 160), and Bar Lounge 808 (see page 54), which has been divided into a daytime and evening space. Those that appear to have developed more from the second strand include the warehouse-style Lux, with its sliding walls, onto which images are projected (similar to New York lounge bar Lot 61) and the curtain-changing Bar Nil (see page 152), with its blank canvas interior for video projections. These design features embrace modern technology. Changing a venue's atmosphere through coloured lights (a development from the halogen days of disco) has become a popular device, as in lounge bar Antidote (see page 42) and in many of the clubs, such as Astro (see page 154), the Bomb and the Supperclub (see page 136). The retractable roof of B 018, changing the space from underground bunker to open-air venue, is by far the most transformational device.

Flexibility is even identifiable in the detail of many designers' work – in many late-night venues, multipurpose furniture functions as seating, tables or dancing platforms. In Float (see page 172), Bar Nil and B 018, seats double as dancing podiums, and at Brown (see page 62) furniture folds away to create more space. At Lux and Soft (see page 76), seating is mobile.

These are flexible times in bar and club design, which is perhaps indicative of the relaxed informality present in many of today's venues, and in particular in late-night and nightclub spaces. Flexibility is also an attempt to provide a venue with a greater shelf-life.

Theatrical Flourishes

If bars and clubs are social arenas where everything is about performance and the patrons are players, then it is no wonder that theatricality as a theme is so often foregrounded. Philippe Starck is a design master of the dramatic gesture and mise-en-scène – in his venues, people feel as though they are on show. One only has to look at Teatriz in Madrid (1990), which was based on one of the city's old theatres, or the more recent Long Bar (see page 104) in London's Sanderson Hotel to recognize this. Starck's tricks are numerous, but his favourite involve playing with proportion, bringing together disparate objects and furniture to create a surreal effect, softening hard surfaces with padded leather, silk or velvet, and using dramatic lighting. Indeed, theatricality can be created in many different ways, for example, through the sheer scale

of a space – take Bernard Khoury's B 018, with its grandeur, its red curtains and its opening roof – or through light – think of another of Starck's creations, the Hudson Hotel Bar, with its disco-style glowing floor, or Jazz Matazz by Jubert-Santacana Architects, where guests are silhouetted against illuminated, amber-coloured light boxes.

Other ways of creating drama involve the arrangement of views and sight lines, and of different heights, so that some people appear almost to be on stage compared with other guests. This is achieved through balconies, mezzanines and differing levels. The late 1970s Manhattan club Studio 54 was created in an old opera house – many clubs of the 1970s were built in old cinemas and dance halls. London's Hippodrome nightclub is on the site of an old theatre dating back to 1900. Other places in the capital, like the Astoria and the Camden Palais, are of a similar ilk. Their modern-day theatricality is literally built-in. Drama can also be found in the elaborate and 'ornate Moorish fantasies' of Ibizan clubs, of which Sheryl Garratt writes, such as Ku and Pacha.

Lighting, heavy drapes and mirrors add to the sense of spectacle in many of today's night-time venues. Consider the mirrored tables of the Purple Bar, the VIP booths in the Mink Bar (see page 112) and colourful drapery and multiple levels of Chinawhite. Man Ray (see page 148), Café l'Atlantique (see page 178) and Float are all fine examples of well-considered, voyeuristic spaces, and,

of course, there is the drama of 'making an entrance', something that Conran, Hobbs & Coppick demonstrated at Quaglino's restaurant in London (1995, on the site of an old ballroom). At the Seagram Brasserie the dramatic entrance is heightened by the use of video cameras, which relay images of arriving guests to the bar. It seems like theatricality is here to stay.

Global Influences

The cross fertilization of ideas is a natural process – the inn was introduced to the New World from Europe and the word 'discothèque' came from France, even if the music danced to was jazz and swing from America. Just like cuisine, multiple global influences can be identified in a designer's work. Morocco has been a favourite theme for a while, the warm palette, comfortable cushions and louche seating providing an attractive style to draw upon.

In London, the restaurant Momo and the basement Kemia Bar pioneered the trend and similar venues can now be found in many towns, like Babaza and Po Na Na and SO.UK. In New York, there is Moomba and Tangerine, both by David Schefer Design, and Miguel Cancio Martins has created several bars with North African styling. Asia is the other strong influence – there are Buddha Bars springing up throughout Europe, Opium and Hakkasan in London and the impressively designed Tao Bistro in Manhattan. Satmoko Ball chose Indonesia as the inspiration for Chinawhite, with Balinese and Chinese details. In keeping with the huge popularity of vodka

as the spirit of choice, most cities now have a Russian
bar, complete with propaganda artwork. Examples range
from Pravda in New York and Dublin to Melbourne's Mink
Bar and London's Babushka.

Many designers are blending foreign and exotic influences
into their interiors without overtly theming them. Starck's
hotel bars place African furniture next to his French Louis
XV furniture; Michael Graves's Miramar Hotel Bar (see
page 102) reflects vernacular architecture; Jeffrey Beers
employs Asian detailing in Float; and Yasumichi Morita
creates contemporary interiors, but uses traditional
Japanese materials (see page 40).

Let us not forget that 'cocktail' or 'style' bars could be
viewed as a global influence, in this case American.
Consider the number of lounges modelled on the New
York style – from Crow Bar (see page 60) and Embassy
in Sydney to Lux in Lisbon. Whether overtly themed, or a
more subtle blend, there is no doubt the design currency
of bars and clubs is global.

Futuristic Forms

If bars and clubs are escapist environments, then it makes
sense that designers often attempt to create unreal
interiors, which transport their inhabitants away from the
everyday world. The invention of synthetic, malleable
materials, such as plastic and fibreglass, meant that
designers in the 1960s like Verner Panton, Ettore Sottsass
and Eero Saarinen could create ergonomic furniture and

objects never possible before. This, together with the
advent of space travel, led to what can be described as
a futuristic design style. The latter part of the 1990s saw
a return to this aesthetic – perhaps the approaching third
millennium had something to do with it – now both retro
and futuristic, or retro-futuro. Although forward-looking,
there was something comfortably familiar about this style
as well, since design, like fashion, tends to develop in a
cyclical way. Perhaps this return is also a kind of
generational nostalgia.

Bars and clubs are ideal spaces in which young designers
can experiment. The life expectancy of a bar is often no
more than three years, so the concern is not to produce a
classic design, but instead, more often than not, to create
a symbol of the times. Retro-futuro or futuristic forms
can be seen in bars all over the world. A good example
is Disney's Encounter bar and restaurant in the old
observation tower at Los Angeles airport, which looks
like a giant H G Wells Tripod. Also worth a mention are
Marc Newson's Pod (1989) in Tokyo and his Mash & Air
restaurant and bar (now closed) in Manchester, UK, for
Oliver Peyton, whose design was developed by Andy
Martin for the restaurant's London site.

Paul Daly's Time (Intergalactic) Beach Bar builds on the
funky, space-age, 2001-meets-Joe-90 aesethetic he
employed earlier at the London bar-restaurant The Saint.
Then, of course, there's Astro, the Bomb and NASA, and
Airconditioned's Soft in Tokyo. Former design partner of

Left:
Momo's Kemia Bar pioneered a
trend in Moroccan-themed
interiors in the UK and elsewhere.

Opposite:
Oliver Peyton's Atlantic Bar & Grill
opened in 1995 and helped
spark London's cocktail bar
revival.

Ron Arad, Alison Brooks's Atoll Bar, on the North Sea island of Heligoland, resembles a mini-spacecraft and even Fabio Novembre's Café L'Atlantique is guarded by Terminator-style android figures. Diller + Scofidio's Seagram Brasserie has elements of a bright future with its gel-moulded seats and Panelite – materials transferred to a new context. Generally, it is late-night clubs that feature such space-age designs, providing an experience that is out of this world.

Lounge Comfort

As technology speeds life up, so it seems many interior designers are attempting to calm people down. A number of them are using neutral, earthy colours, and the cocktail lounge of the 1950s is apparently back. This might be a reaction against the hectic clubs of the early 1990s or symptomatic of the crowded nature of today's cities, where urbanites need a home from home to socialize, their own apartments being too cramped. The move towards increased amounts of seating accommodation in venues that serve alcohol might also be related to the growing number of women partaking in what was once such a male activity. Indeed, throughout the history of bars and drinking places, women have influenced their design. (London's first wine bar was created by a woman architect as an antidote to dark public houses.) Low, relaxed seating, club tubs, sofas and banquettes are all de rigueur in many modern bar and club interiors, so much so, in fact, that United Designers' recent revamp of the Ministry of Sound in London included the creation of a large lounge bar.

Certainly in terms of the projects featured in this book, there is plenty of evidence to suggest that lounge comfort is incredibly popular. Nu Nu Luan's Brown in Hong Kong has a cigar lounge, as does the Mandarin Bar in London (see page 118). Most of design firm Glamorous's projects in Tokyo testify to the rising trend in venues that offer table service (perhaps filtering through from café-bars and hotel bars), with virtually no standing room at all. Once again, it is predominantly the late-night venues that offer these relaxed environments – Embassy, Lux and Float, to name a few. People drink at a far more leisurely pace when they're seated, which perhaps explains why cocktails are often so expensive.

Natural Elements

In terms of the materials that designers have used recently, although those creating more futuristic venues rely on synthetic materials, many are employing wood, leather and marble, either to achieve a timeless, classic look, or simply to ensure longevity. This is especially important with hotel and restaurant bars – the designs of Adam Tihany, David Collins and United Designers all optimize the beauty of natural textures, such as wood grain, onyx, hide and silk. Many other designers look for different ways to incorporate natural elements into their interiors. Obvious examples are the Absolut Icehotel (see page 94) and the use of water in Jeffrey Beers's rumjungle; the aquarium in Lounge 808 and the pool in Man Ray; watery projections in Bar Nil, not to mention the Red Sea Star (see page 50), resting below the waves.

As we rely increasingly on technology, with environmentalists warning of the gradual depletion of our natural resources, designers want to bring the outside, natural world inside. Philippe Starck has stuck a large slab of rock in the Purple Bar as the bar counter; Schefer Design's Leshko's (see page 38) has a bar façade clad in stone; and Nu Nu Luan layers the wood in Brown to make it look like sedimentary rock. Yasumichi Morita uses natural Japanese materials, such as hemp and bamboo, even Michael Young's seemingly futuristic Astro was based on the idea of geothermal properties and the desire to bring Iceland's outside in. Of course, you can't find a better example of the blurring of the boundaries of inside and out than Bernard Khoury's B 018, a venue where the sky is literally the limit.

There are as many designers keen to create classic interiors that are built to last as there are creatives setting out to produce fantastical venues that sparkle for a moment. But whichever the case, the ideas and dreams of bar owners and designers provide lounge lizards, movers and shakers, business and pleasure seekers, schmoozers and boozers and party people around the world with exciting destinations – places to have a drink, strike a deal, kick back and relax, wine and dine, strut their stuff and get lost in music. Bar and club design can offer an escapist realm or a home from home, as you will see in the following pages. When night falls, anything goes.

Bars and restaurant bars

Orbit Bar

Sydney, Australia
Burley Katon Halliday, 1999

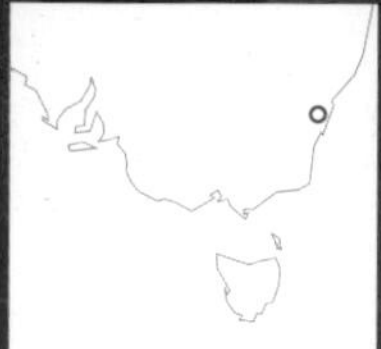

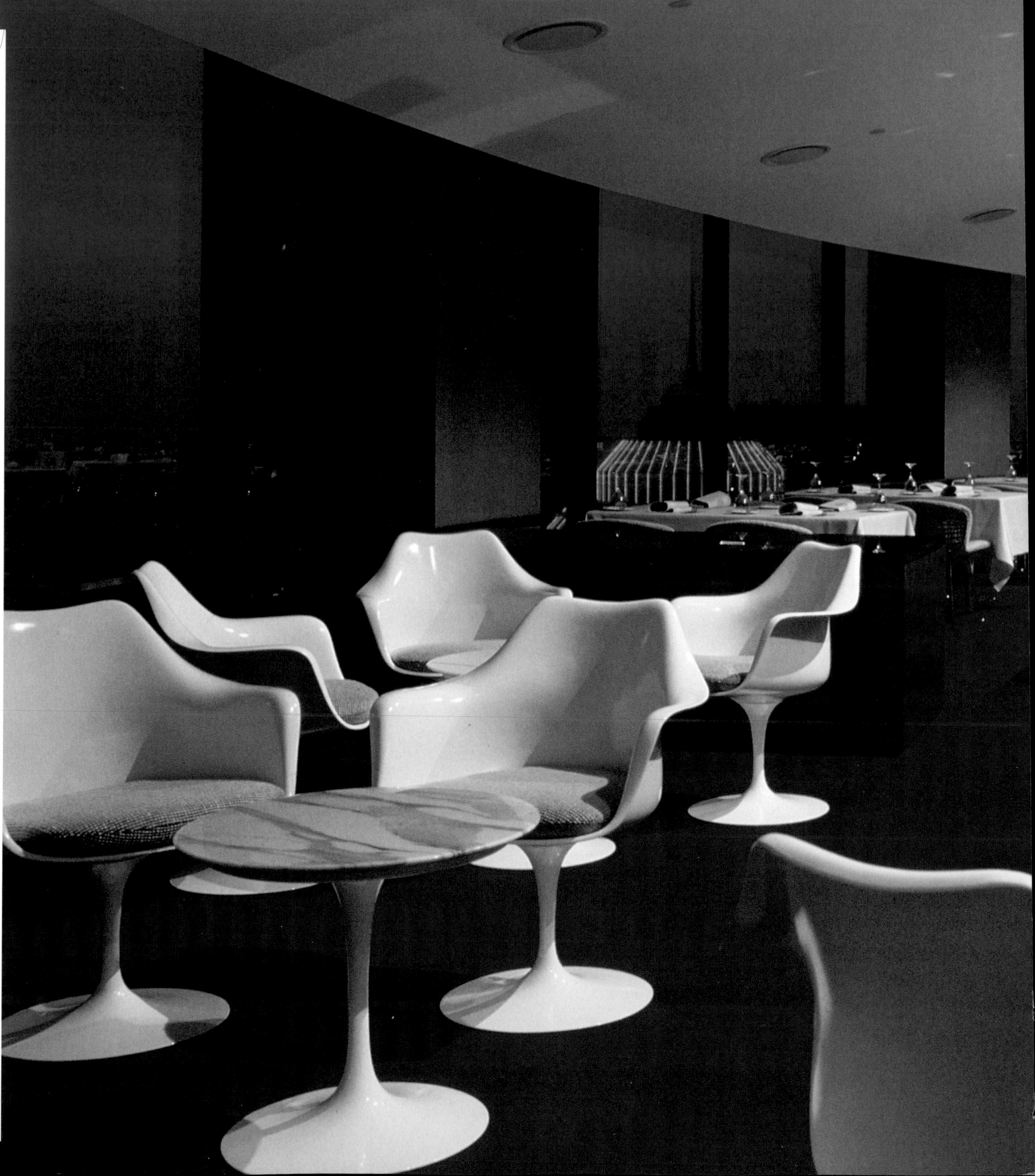

Previous page:
The cockpit-style Orbit Bar is
set on the space's outer revolving
ring, which takes 105 minutes
to complete a full revolution.

Left:
Floor-to-ceiling windows
afford panoramic views of
the Sydney skyline.

Opposite:
Eero Saarinen's Tulip chairs
recapture and revive the spirit
of the 1960s.

Every city should have one – a landmark bar or restaurant that's sky-high with a spectacular 360° view of its urban context. London's revolving restaurant at the top of the Telecom Tower is now defunct, but New York has the Greatest Bar on Earth, Los Angeles is host to Encounter, which is situated in the former observation tower of the city's airport, and in Dublin the Gravity Bar tops the pint glass-shaped atrium at the Guinness Storehouse. The largest, however, is the Summit restaurant in Sydney – the revolving crown of Harry Seidler's award-winning, 48-storey Australia Square Tower, built back in 1969.

30 years later, the hip, modern design team Burton Katon Halliday (BKH), best known for their stylish, boutique hotel The Kirkton, were commissioned to reinvent this 'Sydney dining icon'. Iain Halliday recalls the owner requesting a sensitive refurbishment that would modernize Summit, 'without throwing the baby out and alienating the existing strong clientele' (*Architecture Australia*, March/April 1999). The existing scheme, apparently inspired by Stanley Kubrick's 1968 film *2001: A Space Odyssey*, had several outstanding features that BKH decided were integral and should be retained and strengthened, in order to preserve the essence of the original.

Obviously, the stunning panorama afforded by vast floor-to-ceiling windows is Summit's best asset, especially in conjunction with the circular, split-level layout, which is divided into an outer revolving ring that takes 105 minutes to rotate fully around the stationary, mezzanine core.

BKH ensured these fundamentals remained, enhancing them wherever possible. As Halliday explains: 'We removed elements which disrupted your vision through the interior and out to the view...visual junk. We got rid of all the superfluous clutter and then set up a limited palette of colours and materials, with classic Knoll chairs' (*Architecture Australia*, March/April 1999). So high waiter stations and metal screens that obscured the view were removed, and new additions were set at a lower level and formulated to complement the circular layout.

Although predominantly a restaurant, Summit has the cockpit-style Orbit Bar. A small, curved flight of steps leads down to the bar, which is wedged between dining areas and includes a baby grand piano. As its name suggests, Orbit is set on the rotating, scarlet-carpeted level. A vintage 1960s spirit has been revived by the addition of Eero Saarinen's distinctive, shiny white, fibre-glass Tulip chairs. These are in keeping with the steel-wired Harry Bertoia dining chairs, which have been utilized throughout the dining area. There are also leather banquettes on the inner ring, constructed to face outwards and optimize diners' views. Low lighting makes for an intimate atmosphere, but also allows the dramatic city lights to dazzle and truly steal the scene.

Summit and Orbit are fine examples of retro-futuro – the bold red, white and silver palette and the 1960s forms evoking the technological optimism of that decade, yet at the same time feelings of nostalgia and familiarity.

This, together with new, sophisticated touches – such as the grey terrazzo floor of the inner circle contrasting with the red carpet and the sheer metallic curtain that lines an arc of wall – elevate the interior above a simple refurbishment. BKH have refined the interior – it is stylishly minimal, meeting its purpose to provide the best views of Sydney for the city's high-flyers.

Page

Tokyo, Japan
Yasumichi Morita, 1998

Opposite:
Kondo's uplit chain mail curtain appears as a glowing metallic screen in Morita's mirrored wall.

Right:
The small adjoining bar, seating five, is shielded from the main lounge by chain mail screens.

Far right:
The single shaded lamps appear as twee twin wall-lights in mirror-image.

Sketch:
The bar owner loves books so Morita created two adjoining polished steel walls, with vertical and horizontal slots in which to house the books.

Osaka-born Yasumichi Morita creates glamorous, intriguing interiors through a combination of atmospheric lighting and fascinating materials. Page is a basement lounge bar on the theme of books – not any old books, but visually orientated (read coffee-table) tomes. There is even a tiny snug-cum-gallery, which functions as a showcase for work from *Visionaire* magazine, very appropriate considering the bar's location in Daikanyama, one of Tokyo's most fashionable districts. Page is where the capital's fashionistas and media clique choose to schmooze.

Page is a collaborative work between Yasumichi Morita and Yasuo Kondo, a fellow Japanese interior designer, who specializes in retail design and is best known for his work for Yohji Yamamoto. Instead of working together, they divided the project up, with each of them designing one half of the rectilinear lounge area. In addition, Morita created the Visionaire snug, while Kondo designed the toilets.

Morita chose stainless steel with a mirror finish for his walls, to avoid the feeling of a disjointed interior. He knew that whatever Kondo came up with, it would simply be reflected. The bar owner loves books, so Morita played on the bookshelf concept by creating two adjoining polished steel walls with vertical and horizontal slots in which to house books. The effect is quite unnerving – the books appear to float, their reflections creating the impression that there are even books slotted into the white leather

furniture. Morita's humour manifests itself in his single, shaded lamps attached to the wall, which appear as twee, twin wall-lights in mirror image.

Kondo's chain mail screens complement the 'mirror' wall. In reflection, the uplit metal curtain appears as a glowing metallic wall, adding to the glamorous feel of the lounge. These shiny and illuminated walls, combined with stained black oak flooring and black ceiling, serve to increase the sense of space in the bar, which has a low ceiling. A small adjoining bar set behind the chain mail screens adds to the physical space. When lighting designer Ingo Maurer visited Page, he loved it so much that he donated some of his own freestanding lamps.

Above:
The small snug-cum-gallery functions as a showcase for work from *Visionaire* magazine.

Main image right:
The books appear to float, their reflections creating the impression that there are even books slotted into the white sofas.

Plan:
Guests enter the small bar first, which leads through to the lounge, off which the snug is located.

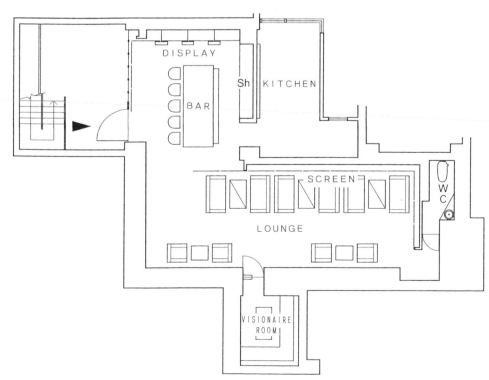

DISPLAY

Sh | KITCHEN

BAR

SCREEN

W C

LOUNGE

VISIONAIRE ROOM

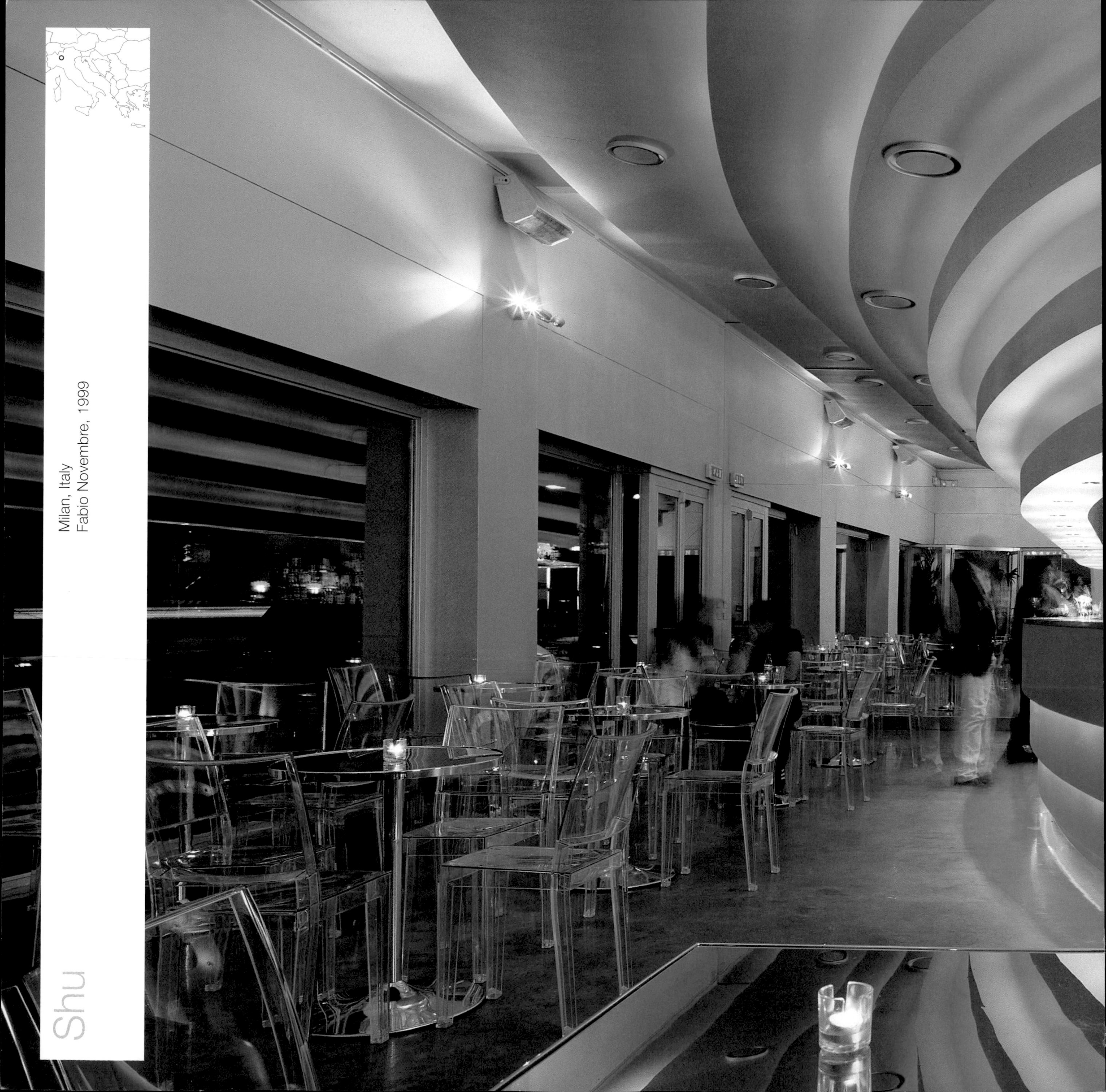

Shu

Milan, Italy
Fabio Novembre, 1999

The concentrically stepped silver bar basks in green neon light, emitted by recessed spotlights in each layer.

Plan
This shows a clear delineation of
space. Patrons enter the bar first
and then, if dining, move through
to the restuarant.

Main image right:
The restaurant's almost
uniformly black interior, in
contrast to the bar, is dominated
by two giant golden forearms –
a representation of the Egyptian
god Shu, who held the
heavens aloft.

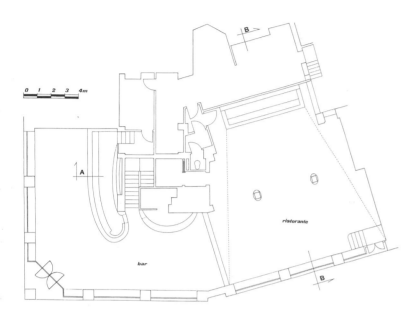

'Be your own Messiah' is designer Fabio Novembre's motto and on his website <www.novembre.it> he describes himself in the following way:

> 'Since 1996, I've responded to those who call me Fabio Novembre.
> Since 1992, I've responded to those who also call me "architect".
> I cut out space in the vacuum by blowing air bubbles, and I make gifts of sharpened pins so as to ensure I never put on airs.
> My lungs are imbued with the scent of places that I've breathed, and when I hyperventilate it's only so I can remain in apnoea for a while.
> As though I were pollen, I let myself go with the wind, convinced I'm able to seduce every thing that surrounds me.
> I want to breathe till I choke.
> I want to love till I die.'

Novembre's sentiments are not dissimilar to those of Brit-artist Damien Hirst, summed up in the title of his monograph *I Want to Spend the Rest of my Life Everywhere, with Everyone, One to One, Always, Forever, Now* (Booth-Clibborn Editions, London, 1997) – they encapsulate a very fin-de-siècle, passionate preoccupation with life and death. However, whereas Hirst uses medical metaphors and cold, clinical imagery to frame his concepts of life and death, Novembre looks to the heavens and opts for glamour and glitz in his interiors, often juxtaposing the fantastical, even the celestial, with technical, quotidian symbolism of the modern world. The restaurant-bar Shu, in Milan, was opened in September 1999 and is a Novembre tour de force.

Guests encounter the bar first, which is dominated by the concentrically stepped silver bar counter, structured like the Guggenheim Museum in New York. Basking in green neon light, it contains spotlights that are recessed within each layer, giving it the overall appearance of a futuristic spacecraft. The grass-green resin floor, transparent plastic tables and reflective table tops serve to enhance the effect. The restaurant is quite a contrast – diners ascend three steps to enter through black velvet curtains, tied back from the walls by silver chains. In the dark space created by the black velvet-padded walls, black-framed dining chairs and the black mosaic-tiled floor, two huge golden forearms shine forth. Each sprouting from inside a crown of spotlights set into the floor, these giant limbs appear to hold up the ceiling and are iconic

representations of Shu – the Egyptian god of the air and atmosphere, who, according to mythology, supported the heavens, holding them aloft, far above the earth.

Instead of heavenly stars, Novembre has created a galaxy of electrical circuits framed in light boxes and arranged in a symmetrical pattern. These glowing green panels cover the entire ceiling, which is built on an incline, sloping down towards a second bar at the end of the restaurant. Framed in stainless steel, the shimmering turquoise bar front is composed of rough-edged glass sheets, back-lit with fibre optics. Either side of this bar area, walls constructed of bullet-proof glass have been riddled with gunshot and, lit from the edges, appear like some haphazard recreation of stellar constellations. Such dramatic effects and theatrical surroundings serve to render diners mere mortals, caught with Shu between heaven and earth.

Opposite:
Black velvet curtains, tied back by silver chains, frame the opening between restaurant and bar. To the right, walls of bullet-proof glass are riddled with gunshot to resemble a stellar constellation.

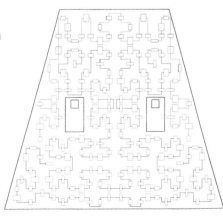

Ceiling plan:
The diagram shows the symmetry of the circuit-like arrangement of light boxes.

Above:
One of the many green light boxes on the ceiling.

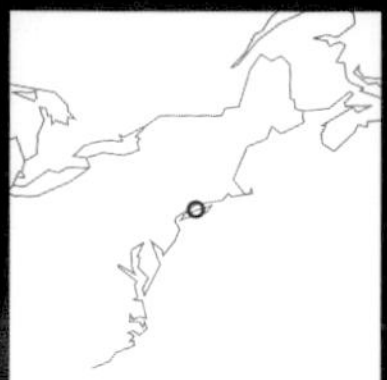

Leshko's

New York, USA
David Schefer Design, 1999

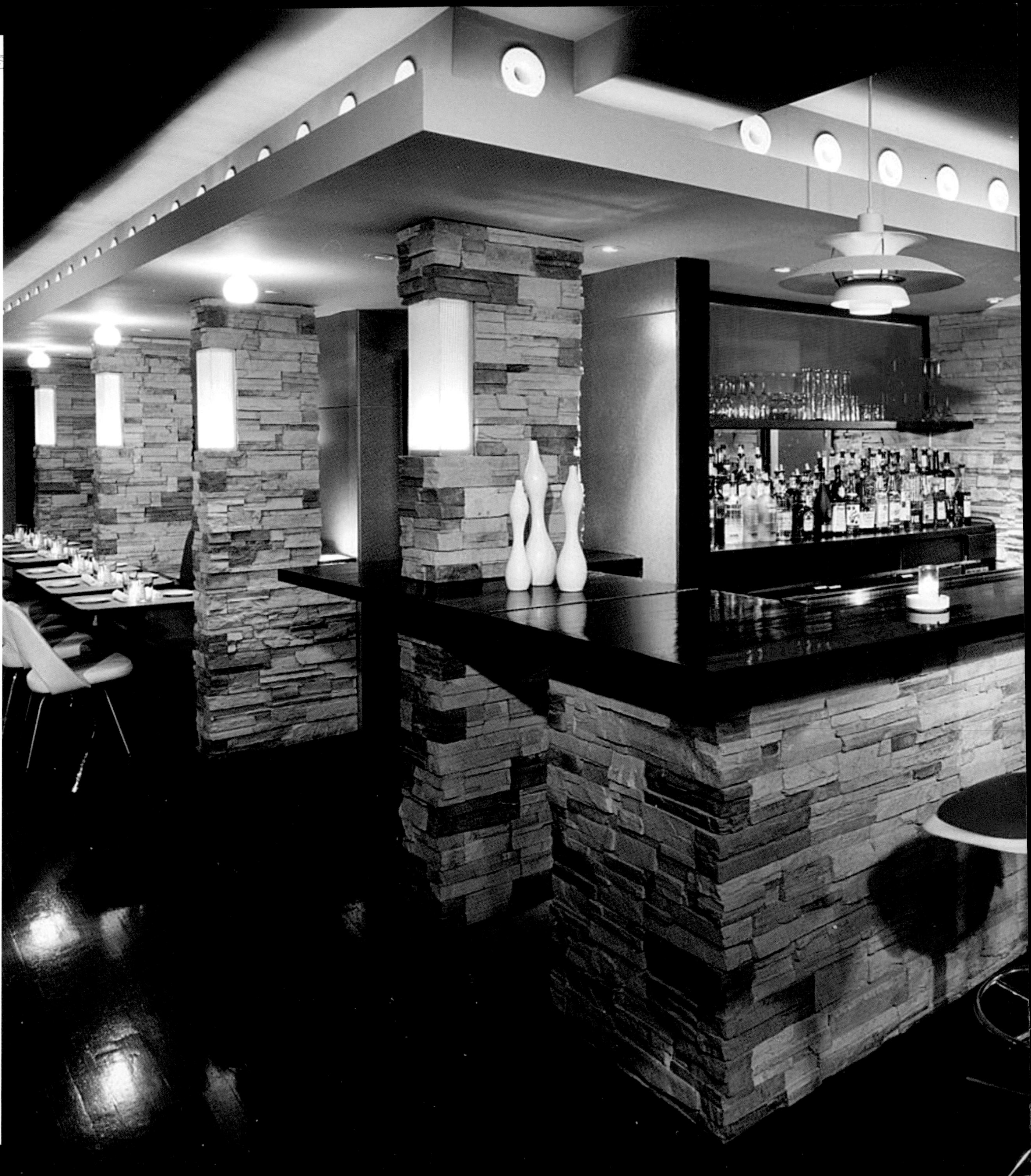

Main image left:
The Flagstone Bar was conceived as a hearth-like, anchoring element. It is the first thing guests see on arrival.

Plan
To expand the space, an L-shape was formed by incorporating a lounge area that had been part of the adjacent building.

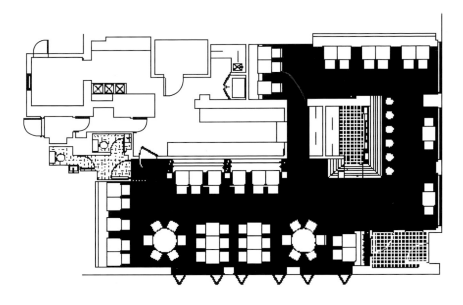

The retro aesthetic of Leshko's is no accident. This cosy, neighbourhood restaurant, created recently by David Schefer and Eve-Lynn Schoenstein, has been remodelled in honour of its namesake – a legendary Ukrainian restaurant, which opened in 1957 on the very same corner in New York's East Village. Leshko's was an eponymously named family affair and apparently thrived up until the late 1970s. A meeting between the present owner and son of the original restaurant owner inspired the brief: 'To create a comfortable neighbourhood gathering spot that would evoke the feeling and spirit of the heyday of the original restaurant.'

The redesign should be considered in the context of the general East Village redevelopment. The once notorious alphabet streets have been up-and-coming for some time and the area surrounding Tompkins Square now offers an eclectic mix of low-rise residential buildings, restaurants, bars and trendy shops. In keeping with the local improvements, the exterior along the side-street façade was transformed by new floor-to-ceiling glass doors, which fold out during the summer months integrating the dining area with the neighbourhood.

David Schefer Design stripped out all elements from the existing restaurant and expanded the space, forming an L-shape by integrating a lounge area that had been part of the adjacent building. The Flagstone Bar is the centrepiece – it connects these two areas and also conceals the kitchen and service points. It is the first

thing that guests encounter as they arrive from the corner entrance. As the designers explain, 'The bar was conceived as a hearth-like "anchoring" element.' The combination of the Poul Henningsen pendant lights, natural-stone cladding, dark-stained wooden bar counter and warm reds of the back bar, a back-lit red acrylic embedded with fabric and seats of the plastic 1950s stools, make the bar an inviting, nostalgic feature.

The colour palette and materials throughout evoke the 'plastic fantastic', post-war and early 1960s period. Pale-toned vintage furniture and wheat-straw board wall panels are enlivened by expanses of strong colour, such as the vibrant-red vinyl banquettes and sky-blue ceiling. There are various lighting sources – recessed lighting, light panels incorporated in the stone-clad columns and back-lit coloured acrylic panels, which bathe the space in shades of yellow and red.

Tsuki-No-Ie

Kobe, Japan
Yasumichi Morita, 2000

Main image left:
The Japanese hemp lampshades create a diffuse light, which is reflected in the bronze mirror of the back bar.

Above left and right:
Customers descending the stairway are drawn to the entrance by a large cube lamp. The restrooms feature a similar lighting installation.

This dining-bar, located in Kobe, Japan, is a fine example of designer Yasumichi Morita's talent for enhancing tiny subterranean spaces through a clever use of lighting and materials. The owner has named it Tsuki-no-Ie, or 'The House of Moon', in celebration of the 'moonlight' quality of the light diffused through the bar's Japanese hemp lampshades.

Morita, who trained as a lighting designer, believes that lighting is the most important element to consider when designing a space. He only employs downlighting to illuminate tabletops for eating and drinking, never to create ambience. Morita says 60 per cent of customers at Tsuki-no-Ie are women and that his main aim is to 'make women look beautiful', hence the soft, tender glow of the standard lamps and hemp light boxes that are set into the bronzed mirror of the back bar.

As customers descend the stairway, they are immediately drawn towards the entrance, which is lit by a large cube light fixture reflected in the pool of water below. To increase the sense of space inside, Morita has created what he calls a 'phantom depth' by inserting a mirrored ceiling and lining the walls with bronze mirror, concealed in part by the bamboo blinds in front of them. Tsuki-no-Ie testifies once again to the designer's belief in using traditional Asian materials in a modern context. The result is a stylish and sharp interior that exudes warmth, generated by the lamplight, bronze walls and earthy textures of the timber floor and furniture.

Antidote

Hong Kong
CPM Asia, 2000

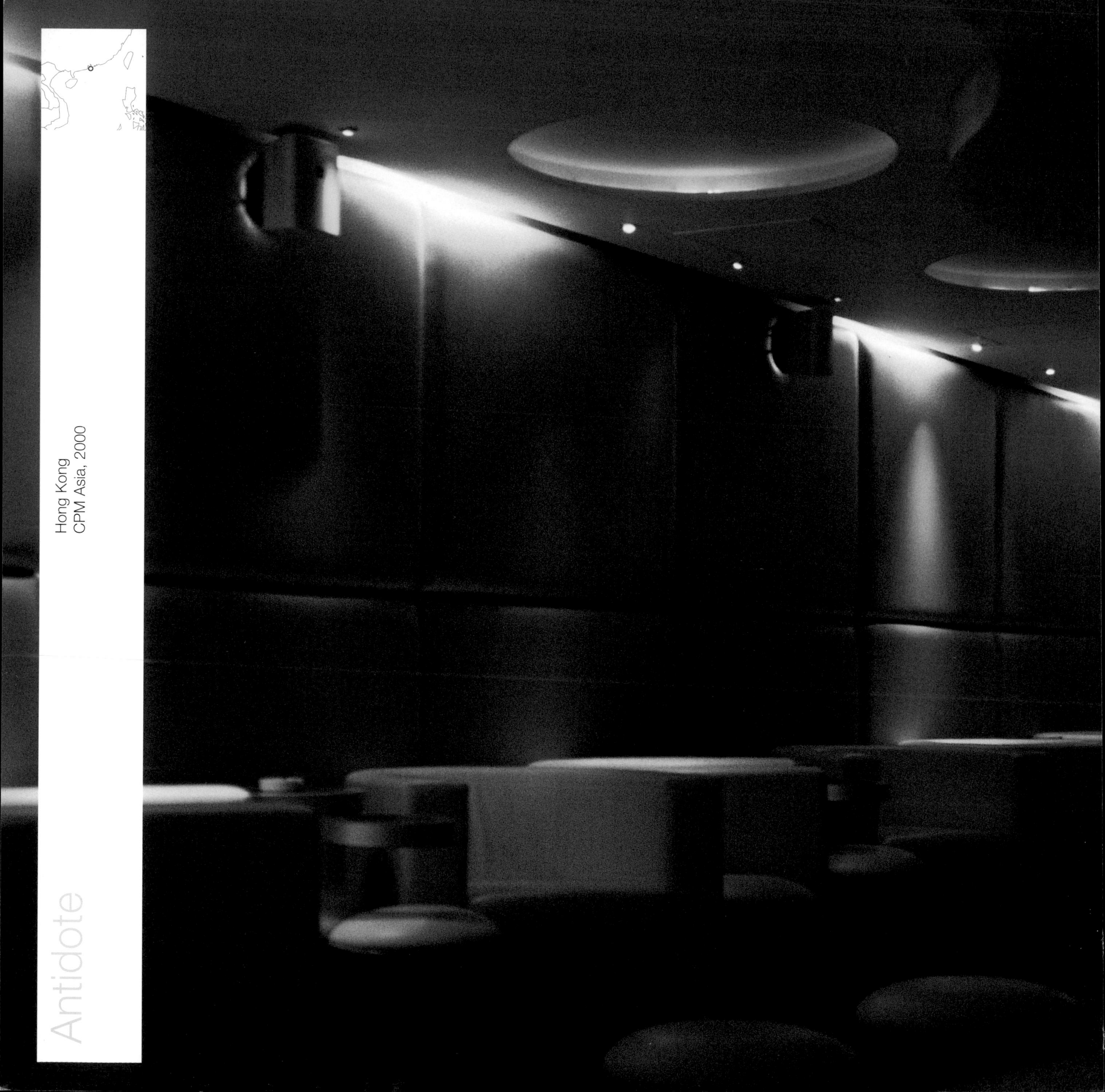

Antidote was conceived in response to fast-paced Hong Kong city life. Simon Chim and John Law of CPM Asia were asked to design a bar where citizens could escape the pressures of the daily grind, somewhere to unwind, relax and lounge. The client specifically requested that the venue be somewhere 'completely anti-Hong Kong', somewhere incredibly comfortable and laid-back, but also luxurious. Inspiration was found in the soft texture and simplicity of a marshmallow – the geometric patterned walls are balanced by the curvaceous shapes and comfortable materials found throughout the long rectilinear space.

Law explains the two basic principles of CPM Asia's concept: 'The first was to create an interior that was as minimalistic as possible without being too stark and the second was to make the interior completely devoid of colours' (*Hong Kong I-Mail*, 28 July, 2000). The result is a white and silver, funky and futuristic cocoon, with padded walls and only the fibre-optic lighting adding a wash of colour. Similar to NASA in Copenhagen, the interior is presented as a 'blank canvas' so that the people are the focus.

Located on a quiet alley in the Central district of the city, a discreet cylinder, sliced diagonally to form a slanted disc, bears Antidote's sign, which is spotlit by the top half above. Passers-by are more likely, however, to notice the distinctive undulating Yin and Yang on the entrance steps that divides the door in half to create a glass panel

Left:
The chunky, white sofa banquette
snakes along one of the walls,
forming booths that look like
oversized Eileen Gray chairs.

revealing a glimpse of the interior. This fluid line continues inside, along the reconstituted marble floor and in the ceiling details – and there is also a long, white vinyl banquette that snakes along one wall. The layout is simple but cosy, without appearing claustrophobic – the oscillating lines soften the corridor-like interior.

Seating levels were kept low to compensate for the restrictive ceiling heights, but they also create a lounge atmosphere. The chunky sofa banquette, with its Michelin Man-like rolls, appears like oversized Eileen Gray chairs, the curves forming intimate booths for groups of people. Conversely, the continuous seating arrangement encourages communication between strangers. Along the opposite wall, white vinyl club chairs are diagonally paired, a circular table with a protruding ring devised to hold the white resin champagne buckets positioned between each pair.

In order to create an feeling of volume and depth, CPM Asia played with the ceiling levels. The curved silver layer above the sofa conceals air-conditioning units, but also creates a greater sense of height in the remaining half of the room. The circles cut in the gypsum board ceiling perform the real tricks on the eyes – each successive circle from the door to the bar is smaller in size, creating a feeling of depth through false perspective. These circular coffers are uplit from their edges in various neon shades, suffusing the room with different colours. At the far end, the bar curves softly into the space, which, constructed

from white and aluminium laminate, soaks up the various lighting colours, as does the white marble bar top. The white and aluminium laminate chequerboard end wall conceals all bottle storage and bar equipment, thus maintaining the simple, clean purity of the space.

Above:
Circular cut-outs in the ceiling are
lit by neon lights that change
colour, adding dynamism to the
predominantly white interior.

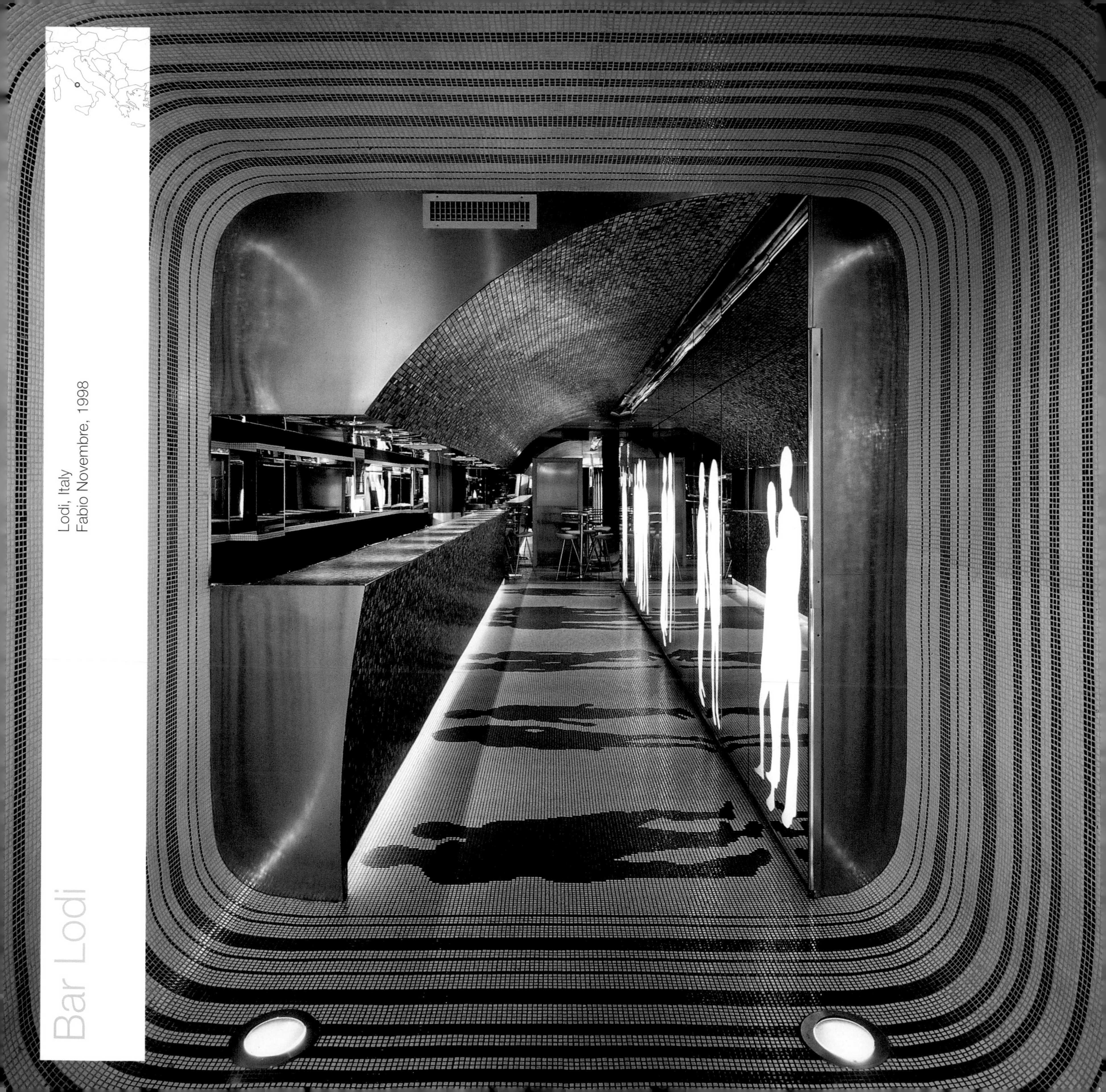

Bar Lodi

Lodi, Italy
Fabio Novembre, 1998

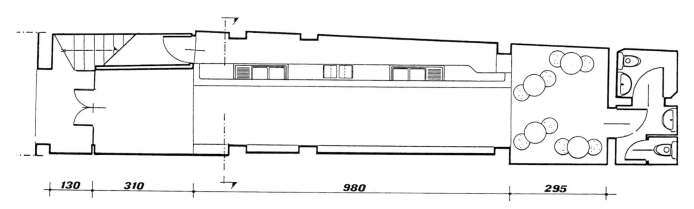

| 130 | 310 | 980 | 295 |

Bar Lodi may be one of Fabio Novembre's simplest and smallest interiors, but it nonetheless exhibits the same themes and preoccupations that are more readily identifiable in his grander projects. The tunnel-like entrance, with its rounded corners, displays a monochromatic tiled design in the form of Bisazza's Opus Romano mosaic, which is a magnified replica of the bar code of Novembre's book, *A Sud di Memphis* (Idea Books, Milano 1995). The concentric black lines frame the bar area beyond and two floor spotlights guide the eye inwards, like an airport runway or fashion show catwalk. The fluorescent light recessed below the bar façade to the left and the mirror reflection of the top right recessed light, further emphasize this dynamic perspective.

Designing the space proved to be problematic, as Novembre explains: 'The main problem was to have a very long and narrow space, so the aim was to ideally open it, break it, through reflection effects.' The result was mirror lining the entire length of one wall, thus amplifying the space by reflecting the tunnel-like form of the bar opposite. Plaster-cast moulded panels form the curved façade of the lower bar and the arched ceiling above; they are coated in Bisazza's Vetricolour mosaic, which features warm shades of copper, gold and brown. The black-and-white bar code design is repeated at the end of the bar in the small seated area, which has tables from Amat and stools designed by Carlo Mollino.

The illuminated figures were created by scratching the silver from the mirror and adding fluorescent back-lighting. As Novembre comments, 'All this, besides solving the lighting needs, gives a sense of presence of people even when the bar is empty.' The perfect shadows on the floor, made from black mosaic tiles, correspond to the mirror figures, which were taken from a 1969 photograph by Richard Avedon of members of Andy Warhol's Factory in New York. It is perhaps no coincidence that Novembre chose this dialogue with Warhol, an artist also concerned with mortality – remember, we are all famous for 15 minutes.

We may indeed feel that Bar Lodi is full when it is empty; full of Novembre's obsession with life, energy and architecture. As he told *Frame* magazine (No. 9, 1999), 'Architecture is the last medium to acknowledge that we're made of flesh and blood, that in the end there's only us, that we're surrounded by the tangible, by people we can't touch, embrace, take to bed.'

The ghostly white, illuminated figures were taken from a 1969 photograph by Richard Avedon of Andy Warhol's Factory members in New York. Their shadows are laid in black mosaic tile on the floor.

Main image left:
The bar stools float like technicolour jellyfish – spotty seats supported by metal tentacles – and above a starfish-shaped 'Starlight' shields guests from direct downlighting.

Above:
Coral lamps, fabricated from silk and metal, cling like anemones to the ceiling, amongst strange pebble shapes, which are made from soundproof foam.

The Red Sea Star restaurant and bar is underwater and out of this world. Only the steel walkway leading to a jetty 90 metres (300 feet) offshore is visible from above sea level. However, 6 metres (20 feet) below, amongst the coral and fauna, the Red Sea Star exists with an interior that mirrors the liquid life thriving outside its windows. This mini-Atlantis is a completely new build and forms part of a larger project by architect Josef Kiriaty in Eilat, Israel. It was completed in January 1999 by Ayala Serfaty and her Tel Aviv-based company Aqua Creations. Serfaty's aim was 'to balance the experience of floating weightlessly in the water with the stable feeling of being safe on shore'.

It is accessed via two lifts, one for guests and the other for food – the toilets and kitchens are above sea level. The restaurant comprises three dining wings, which lead off the main area, seating 100 diners in total. The bar is located in a fourth wing to the rear of the restaurant. The entire space is submerged and surrounded by water, like some stranded submarine, 62 windows providing a panorama of the sea life beyond. These curvy panes of glass radiate a blue light, but table tops of deep coral orange and lighting of the same colour lift the interior out of the blue. As Serfaty comments, 'I balanced the blue using warm tones in the lighting and furniture. The final colour composition is very complete and harmonious.'

All furniture and lighting, except for the dining chairs, were produced by Aqua Creations and display the 'organic aesthetic' that has become their design signature. Serfaty

Opposite:
The 'wet sea sand' floor of epoxy resin creates mellifluous reflections of aquatic forms above.

Above left:
Only the steel walkway leading to a jetty 90 metres offshore is visible above sea level.

Above right:
The entire space is under water, like a grounded submarine; 62 windows bring the liquid life of the ocean in.

trained as a sculptor and treats each product as a sculptural work. She says, 'It is important to me that the works project warmth. The image in my head is an object that gives you a welcome hug when you arrive home.' Certainly in the context of the Red Sea Star they appear like aquatic life forms – coral lamps fabricated from silk on metal cling like anemones to the ceiling amongst flattened pebble shapes (made from soundproof foam covered in felt) and modified versions of Serfaty's Margarita tables appear to sprout like flowers from the floor.

The interior is almost cartoon-like – there isn't a straight line in sight. Window frames are curved, support columns are disguised by silk-on-metal structures that stretch upwards, like tall water reeds. The odd appearance of Starlights, delicate silk-and-metal starfish, suspended to shield guests from direct downlighting, adds a sense of discovery. The bar stools float like technicolour jellyfish – spotty upholstered seats supported by metal tentacle legs. Coral walls divide the dining areas and barnacled surfaces soften edges, corners and angles where side tables or counter tops meet walls. The barnacle effect is created by imprinting small shells one by one and by hand, into the sawdust-and-resin surface. It is the 'wet sea sand' floor and shiny table tops that add the magic touch, though; these epoxy resin surfaces create mellifluous reflections of the organic forms emerging from the deep blue of the sea above, while the surface beneath the diners' feet ripples with images of aquatic life, creating the illusion of walking on water, while underwater.

Main image left:
The U-shaped bar is the main feature of the bright, silvery café-bar and mirrors the room's wedge shape.

Plan:
The triangular site is divided into two areas – a café-bar at the front, open from midday, and a smaller cocktail lounge called the Chestnut Room, at the back.

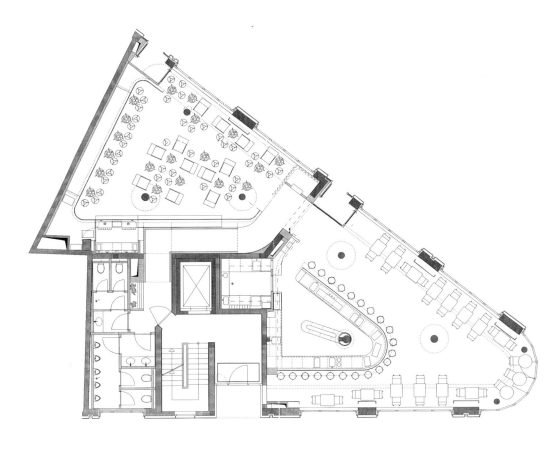

Bar Lounge 808 is situated in Mitte, the Berlin district that has fast become, since German reunification, an exciting mix of art galleries, designer boutiques, delis, bars, cafés and restaurants. Most places are created on small budgets, DIY-style by their owners. That is, until the sophisticated Bar Lounge 808 arrived on the scene. American Bob Young commissioned Alexander Plajer and Werner Franz to design a '1960s-style bar/lounge that would recall an era of US socializing, when going out for a drink meant dressing up, when men knocked back martinis at gleaming long bars and ladies sipped Manhattans on sofas low enough to show off their legs.' Like many modern, stylish cocktail lounges, Bar Lounge 808 was intended to accommodate professionals in the fashion, art, entertainment and dot.com industries, plus ex-clubbing 'thirtysomethings'.

In executing their brief, Plajer & Franz concentrated on the natural elegance of 1960s design, rather than the kitsch, psychedelic aesthetic of the decade. As Plajer says, 'It was, of course, a period that used a lot of beautiful, refined woods and filigree metal supports to create an impression of lightness and levity. It achieved an element of subtle elegance that is very comfortable and light.' Not that light was a problem – Bar Lounge 808 occupies a wedge-shaped, corner site, with floor-to-ceiling windows forming a 40 metre (131 foot) glass façade. In fact, the interior proved to be too 'open' and overexposed, so diaphanous, sheer curtains were chosen to line the windows. These tempt and awaken a sense of curiosity

in passers by, providing guests with a sense of escapism, whilst retaining a connection with the city outside. In summer, the curtains are drawn back and housed in wooden niches (concealed behind the wood panelling) and the windows open back, allowing the tables and chairs to spill out onto the pavement, forming an impromptu terrace area.

The triangular site was divided into two areas – a café-bar at the front, open from midday, and an evening cocktail lounge called The Chestnut Room, at the back. Although the spaces are very different, the lounge is more enclosed and exudes golden tones, whereas the café-bar is silvery and brighter. Both are thematically connected by the wood panelling. The geometric design was inspired by 1960s stone relief, but crafted from sandblasted larch. As Plajer & Franz explain, 'We wanted the structure of hard annual rings to remain visible, but we couldn't let women rip runs into their stockings when sitting at the bar. It was one of the biggest challenges: how can we treat the wood so no one leaves with a splinter?' So they stained and finished it with wax, making it smooth and tactile, yet retaining the natural warmth and 'velvet quality' of the wood. The smoked oak flooring, sealed with oil, also serves to connect the spaces.

The U-shaped bar, measuring 20 metres (66 feet) in length, is the main feature of the café-bar and mirrors the room's wedge shape. It is highlighted by opaque pendant lights and recessed lighting, which radiates a U-shaped

Main image right:
The bar is framed by sandblasted
larchwood panelling, which bears
a geometric pattern inspired by
1960s stone relief.

Previous spread:
Diffuse lighting bathes the
evening cocktail lounge – The
Chestnut Room – in a sunny
warmth, intensified by the wood
and golden hues.

Sketch:
An early sketch shows the
Chestnut Room, with low lounge
chairs and the aquarium
adjoining the bar hatch.

halo from the ceiling panel above. A wide band of
stainless steel forms the bar counter elevation, topped by
small golden-brown and bronze-coloured glass mosaic
tiles, which are also used on the table tops. Aside from
the bar stools, the café furniture is arranged around the
perimeter of the room, lining the windows. All furniture
framework has been powder-coated in silver to
correspond with the metallic theme – at its most
prominent in the lacquered wallpaper on the structural
support columns. 'We thought long and hard about what
to do with the supports. Do we leave them naked, or
dress them up? We liked the idea of metallic wallpaper,
which has a long tradition in Germany. We opted for a
light pattern of lines, which were a popular theme in the
60s and have a thinning effect that adds elegance. Lines
also wouldn't compete with the strong statement of the
wall panels.

The Chestnut Room is a far more louche affair. Diffuse
lighting creates warmth and the wood and metallic hues
reflect and intensify the effect. As in the café-bar, the
metal framework of the furniture is powder-coated, this
time in gold. The unusual 'bubble' table tops are made
from brass discs welded together, with a clear finish
applied to prevent oxidization. A 2.5 tonne aquarium,
measuring almost 5 metres (16 feet) in length, provides a
relaxing focal point. Encased in the wood panelling, it is a
visual continuation of the small bar hatch. The illuminated
tank also affords guests passing through the corridor to
the restrooms a watery glimpse of the space.

Crow Bar

Auckland, New Zealand
Issenbel Architects, 1998

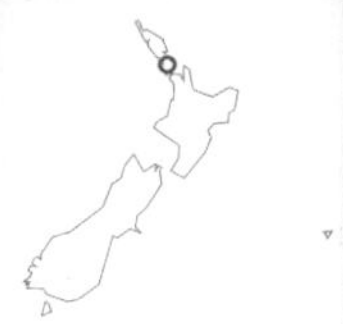

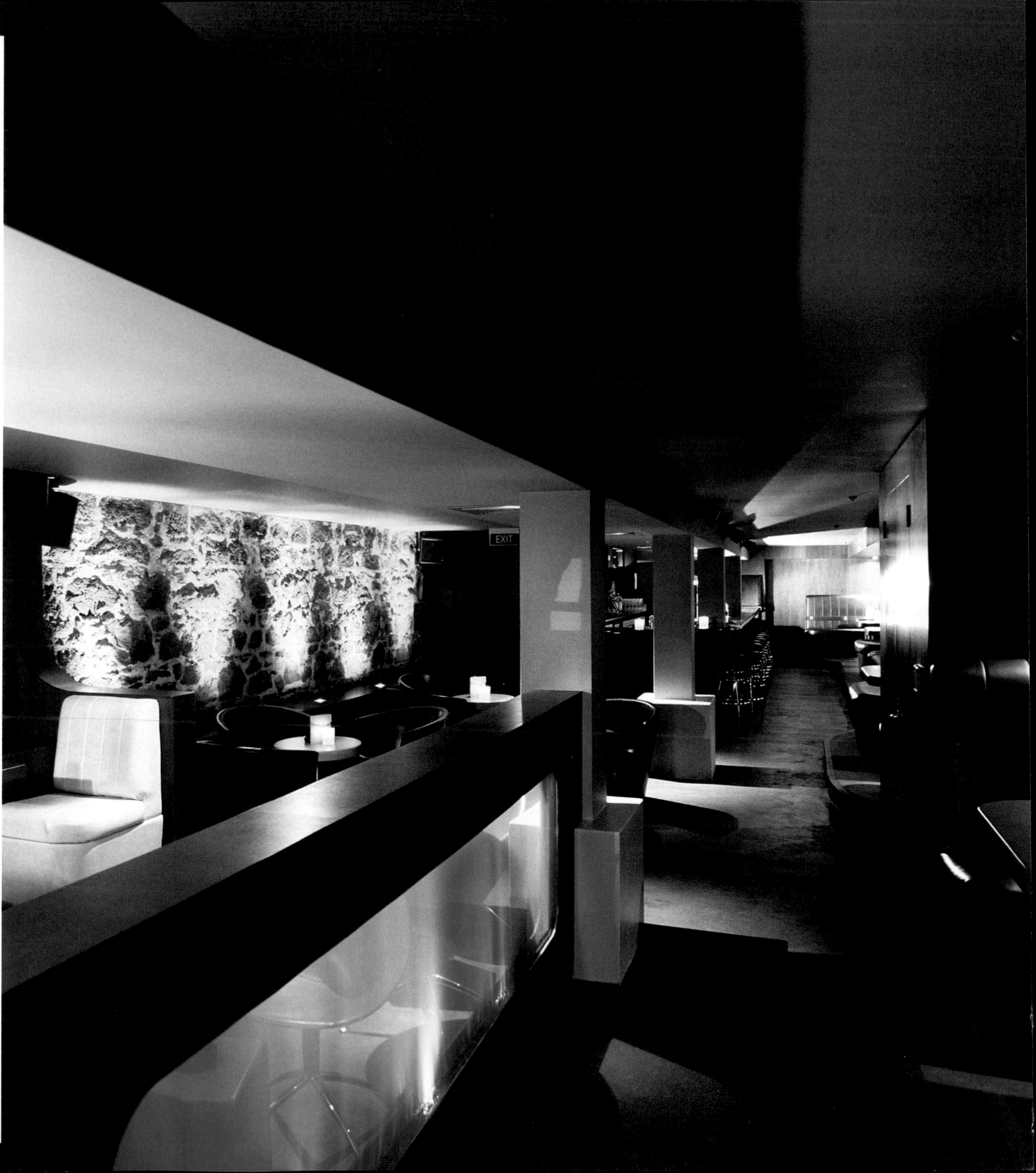

Opposite:
A bubbling wall of water, lit
in electric blue, separates
the entrance corridor from
lounge areas.

Right:
The narrow basement was
made more welcoming by the
addition of continuous snaking
banquette seating.

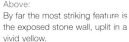

Above:
By far the most striking feature is
the exposed stone wall, uplit in a
vivid yellow.

Although the architects responsible for the refurbishment of the Crow Bar intended to create an interior with a 'timeless aesthetic', there is no doubt that, at least in theory, this late night lounge bar is very much rooted in the present. Not only has there been a re-emphasis of late on natural, durable materials, such as leather, stone and wood panelling, but also a revival of cocktail lounge culture as the new glamorous alternative to pubs or clubs. As the demand for martinis and mojitos sweeps through the world's major cities – New York, London, Sydney, Tokyo, etc. – so it reaches Auckland, New Zealand.

Crow Bar was formerly a nightclub of dubious repute, closed down, allegedly, for drugs activity on the premises. The new owner has resurrected the venue as a lounge bar with de luxe leather booths and acres of wood, a sophisticated setting for cocktails and cigars. The drinks list even features liquid tributes to those legendary New York bars the Stork Club and Rainbow Rooms, places that served cocktails the first time around. Sarah Shand of Issenbel Architects was asked to transform the long, narrow basement, which she describes as 'a dark, dingy concrete bunker, embedded in downtown Auckland...with no articulated or defined areas', into a warm, welcoming space. Hence the continuous snaking banquette stretching along one side, forming chunky rib-backed booths, set against richly grained wood panelling.

The exposed stone wall is by far the most dramatic feature, uplit by vivid yellow spotlights (waterproof halogen fittings, with coloured diffusers) that are set into a ledge. The wall's raw texture contrasts starkly with the muted tones of the leather furnishings. Additional seating is provided by red, Italian leather chairs and cream leather seats, arranged either side of narrow drinks shelves, which are cantilevered to appear as though they fold up. Lighting is used theatrically elsewhere, like at the entrance to the bar, where a wall of bubbling water radiates electric blue light, acting as a screen to separate the lounge area from the entrance corridor.

The actual bar is located at the far end of the space, opposite the booths. There is a second bar upstairs, accessible only from the main basement bar. Like many great subterranean drinking dens, the Crow Bar exhibits no grand neon signage, but has simply an engraved plate set into the floor of the entrance, so if you decide to join Auckland's lounge lizards and fly-by-nights, keep your eyes to the ground.

Hong Kong
Nu Nu Luan, 1999

Opposite:
Metallic silk fabrics form a soft ceiling in the cigar library. When lit from above, it has the effect of sunlight streaming through.

Right:
The bar counter has been constructed from layers of different woods, like the sedimentary strata of a cliff face.

During the 1990s, there was a brief return to the home – for many young people, staying in was apparently 'the new going out'. A consequence of this, in terms of bar and restaurant design, was the emergence of a new lounge aesthetic offering cosier environments that were distinct from the grand, über-creations of the 1980s. Many such lounges can be found in densely populated cities like New York, where apartments are notoriously small. Brown, which opened in 1999, is a perfect example of this trend – a local hang-out in Happy Valley, a quiet, leafy district in one of the world's busiest cities, Hong Kong. Architect Nu Nu Luan created Brown in her own neighbourhood.

In an attempt to emulate the home, environment designers often organize commercial interiors into different sections. Brown is no exception. There are three separate areas – a dining room, lounge and garden veranda. The venue is multi-purpose, yet on an intimate scale. Luan's inspiration came from her passion for whiskey, which soon became an adverb: 'Shall we go brown tonight?' was a familiar phrase amongst her and her friends. Brown offers products that are an extension of this love, with an emphasis on goods that come from the earth, like single malt whiskies aged in wooden casks, coffee and cigars.

Luan chose warm, 'earthy' natural materials to create a familiar, comfortable environment. Slate stone and timber floors, suede furniture and plenty of wood, including American walnut and the big 1990s favourite African wenge. The bar has been constructed from

layers of different coloured woods, like a cliff face showing various sedimentary strata. The bar counter is wrapped in leather and topped with glass. In the cigar library, which includes a built-in humidor, metallic silk fabrics form a soft ceiling. When lit from above, it appears as though sunlight is streaming through the silk; when lit from below, the light reflects off the fabric, casting a warm, copper glow over the lounge.

Furniture has been devised with flexibility in mind – banquettes fold up against the wall, sofas are in modular sections and stools double as coffee tables. Brown appears very much a part of the neighbourhood. Mirrors reflect the street outside and in summer the glass doors at the front fold up and the pavement becomes a café terrace. The courtyard, with cypress trees and teakwood furniture, is a quieter alternative. 'Going brown' has proved so popular there is now a second one in the Mid-Levels district of the city.

rumjungle

Las Vegas, USA
Jeffrey Beers International, 1999

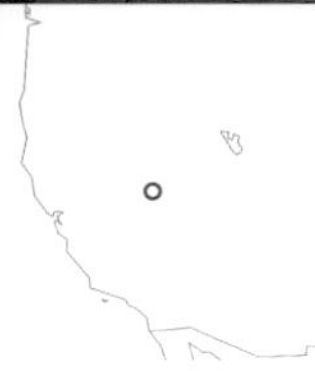

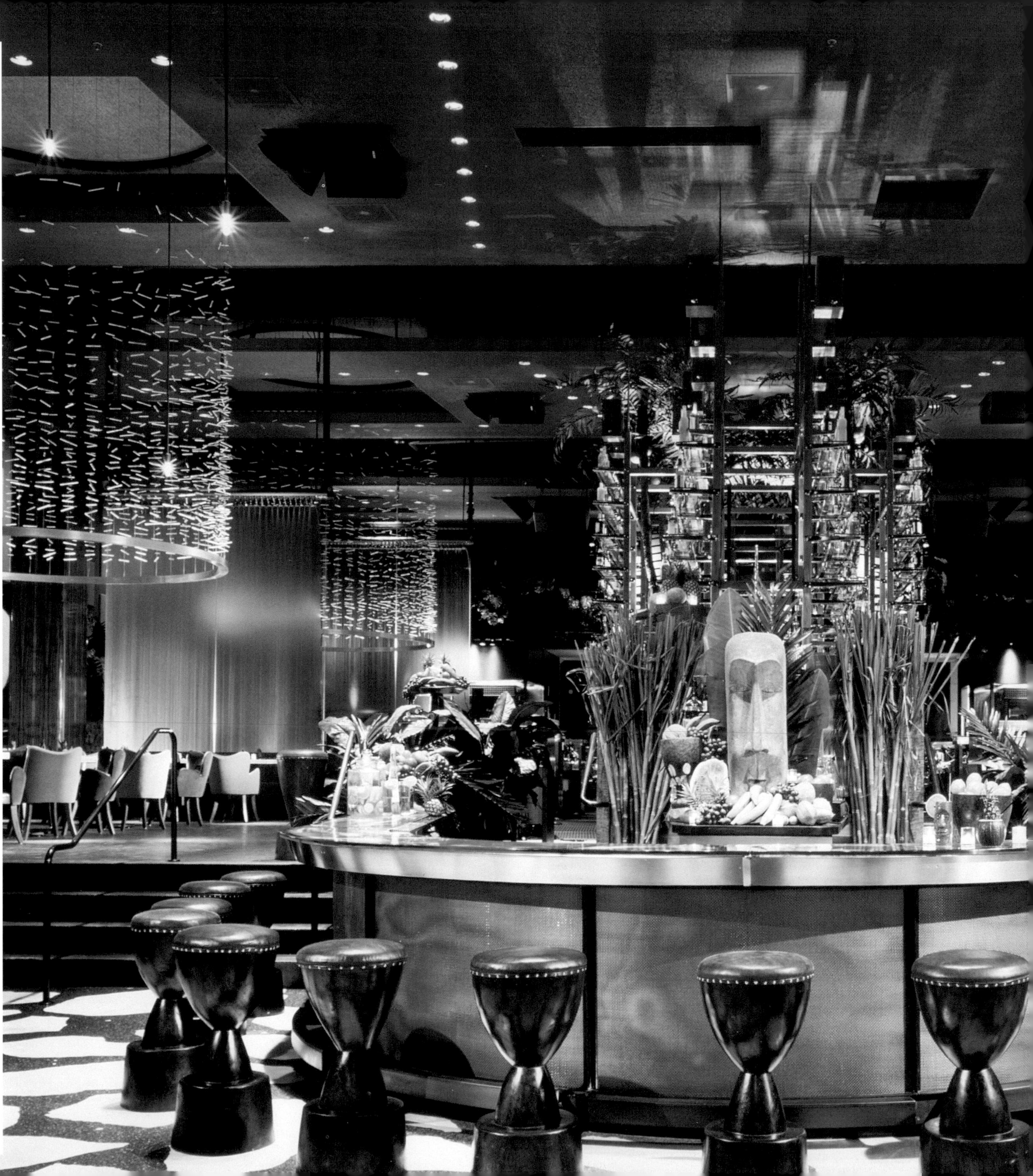

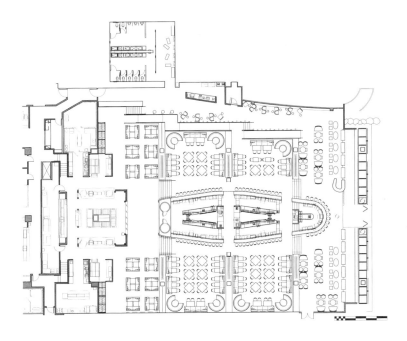

rumjungle offers a visual feast of tropical colours and textures. Like a natural rainforest, there is a bewildering array of forms and shapes, which are arranged to excite and entice patrons. Measuring 2,320 square metres (25,000 square feet), it opened in March 1999 and took Jeffrey Beers International five months to complete. The design of the venue, located in Mandalay Bay, Las Vegas, is based on a jungle theme, as Jeffrey Beers International explain: 'Our challenge was to create a restaurant/nightclub based upon an equatorial regional food and music concept. We created rumjungle to reflect the depths of a mystical jungle…a stepped landscape, flowing water, flaring fire and a temple to the gods.'

As a design concept, rumjungle is well organized. Its simple layout places the large Mountain of Rum Bar as the centrepiece, surrounded by the restaurant. However, the rectangular space has been extremely carefully considered with various themes and motifs contributing to the creation of the jungle aesthetic. There are three sections representing a movement from cool to hot and defined spatially by a gradual ascension or stepping of levels. These 'landscapes', organized along a central axis, are the Fire/Water Pylon Wall, the Mountain of Rum and the Exhibition Kitchen towards the rear.

The steel-framed façade that is the Fire/Water Pylon Wall is spectacular, with its concrete and plaster panels appearing like huge blocks of stone, similar to those of an ancient temple. The glass gaps in the wall reveal 160

Main image left:
The Mountain of Rum Bar is the centrepiece of the space. The acrylic bar is surrounded by drum-shaped, leather-topped stools, carved from Balinese sugarwood.

Plan:
rumjungle is arranged over three stepped levels and organized along a central axis, culminating in the Exhibition Kitchen.

flickering torches and either side of the entrance flames burn inside steel display boxes, which spell out 'rumjungle'. The open doorway frames the Mountain of Rum bar beyond. Dripping with foliage and topped with a stone masthead, it is perfectly centred like some kind of sacrificial altar or place of worship. Once inside, guests are offered the flip side view of the firewall, a floor-to-ceiling glass wall cascading with water – an effect that is repeated in the restaurant area.

The Mountain of Rum island bar is the first thing guests encounter and it is the main focus of rumjungle. It is formed, almost literally, from a mountain of rum – 5,000 bottles stacked up to the pepper red ceiling. The curved acrylic bar counter is surrounded by drum-shaped, leather-upholstered stools, carved from Balinese sugarwood. This initial area appears exotic and earthy, with simple timber furniture, bronze tables, terrazzo and onyx flooring, reminiscent of animal hide, tropical fruit and ferns.

The next layer is the restaurant, which surrounds the Mountain of Rum bar. Rectangular waterwalls divide the restaurant into four more intimate dining sections. These opaque screens break up the space and diffuse the light beautifully. Each segment is crowned by a bespoke 'rain chandelier', constructed from small aluminium tubes attached to wire. This cylindrical mobile continues the water theme, the tubes reflecting the rays from the fibre optics contained within the chandelier, similar to the way

in which raindrops catch sunlight as they fall from the sky. Beyond the restaurant, the design returns to the fire theme with the Exhibition Kitchen, a square structure clad in red metal planks like an inferno, or temple of fire. A pair of colossal, black-and-white striped conga drums, which are elevated by hydraulics, signal the division between the Mountain of Rum and Exhibition Kitchen. Guests can escape the tropical climate in the restrooms, where fibre optics set into the vaulted ceiling appear like stars.

Opposite:
Waterwalls divide the restaurant into four dining sections, each one dominated by a 'rain chandelier'.

Above:
The steel-framed façade features concrete and plaster panels that resemble the huge stone blocks of an ancient temple.

The Brasserie
Seagram Building

The basement brasserie has a certain airiness due to a combination of the diffuse lighting, the white, classic 1950s chairs and the translucency of the back bar and pale-green resin table tops.

The Brasserie is set deep in the stone basement of the Seagram Building, Mies van der Rohe's classic golden and glass, 38-storey office tower in midtown Manhattan, New York. Architectural firm Diller + Scofidio were commissioned to renovate the space, following a fire in 1995 that destroyed Philip Johnson's original 1959 restaurant interior. As Diller + Scofidio themselves say, 'The prospect of redesigning one of New York's legendary restaurants in one of the world's most distinguished modernist buildings was as inviting as it was daunting.'

Although they had never created a restaurant before, Diller + Scofidio's design captures succinctly the social, theatrical and glamorous spirit of modern dining in a world city. The existing concrete shell has been re-lined with new layers, like 'the restoration of an old coat with new skins'. Pearwood ceiling panels wrap down around the main dining space, not only providing seating at both ends, but also accommodating lighting. Each pearwood layer overlaps the last, diffusing the light from the spotlights embedded in the preceding panel, and in doing so highlighting the natural wood. The translucency of the pale-green, resin table tops, the white, classic 1950s chairs and the bar elevate the solid wood panelling and chunky booths – large, L-shaped slabs, upholstered in green leather.

As a completely new addition, the Champagne Bar plays an important role within the Brasserie. Project leader Charles Renfro explains: 'It works both as a place for

Left:
Unusual materials were chosen to create unique effects, such as the illuminated Panelite back bar, which makes the wine bottles appear blurry and two-dimensional, and the bar stool seats, moulded from a medical gel that always matches the occupant's body temperature.

Opposite:
The design engages with the ideas of theatricality and 'making an entrance' – from the LCD screens above the bar, displaying guests as they arrive, to the catwalk-like staircase that leads down to the centre of the space.

drinking and dining, and as a pivot between the front and back dining rooms.' Positioned along one wall of the main dining room, most of the 9 metre (30 foot) long bar counter functions in a traditional 'bartended' way, but the stone bar top is cantilevered, so that it extends partially across the opening between the two dining rooms. This arrangement allows those on bar stools in the main dining room to sit opposite their drinking companions, seated on the bartender's side of the counter, but also creates another row of seats in the second room at a narrower drinking shelf, which faces the central space. The bar thus redefines a transitional area by making it social, voyeuristic and interactive – there is the communal drinking area, but also a more passive body of onlookers. At the end of the bar, a spun aluminium 'vase', inserted into a hole in the counter top, stretches down to the floor, containing an appropriately sculptural floral decoration.

Other aspects of the bar are formative of the Brasserie experience. Much of Diller + Scofidio's design engages with the theatrical notions of dining and, more specifically, the drama of 'making an entrance'. A sensor-activated video camera takes a freeze-frame shot of every new arrival as they pass through the revolving doors into the reception. These images are then beamed to barflies on the LCD monitors that 'float' above the bar. 15 patrons are chronicled in a row, each new arrival replacing the previous one by moving one screen to the right before

vanishing completely. As Renfro explains, 'This has all sorts of voyeuristic connotations; it's good if you're waiting for your date, or if you want to avoid someone.'

This visual drama of the 'entrance' continues. Guests enter the dining room through a doorway in the pearwood wall and then descend a catwalk-like staircase, encased by glass balustrades, that leads down into the centre of the space. Arrivals and departures aside, it is the glowing back bar that is the most striking feature of the dining room – the wine bottles on display appear to float. It is constructed from a material called Panelite, a corrugated honeycomb of aluminium with translucent facing panels. Acid-etched glass doors appear in front. When backlit, the bottles stored inside appear blurry and two-dimensional – as objects can appear if you've had one drink too many.

The curvy seats of the bar stools are moulded from a honey-like medical gel produced in Italy, with stainless steel bases custom-designed by Diller + Scofidio. The gel possesses a special thermal property, which always matches the occupant's body temperature. Although making an entrance at the Brasserie is apparently effortless, with a bar like this, departing is, no doubt, more of a struggle.

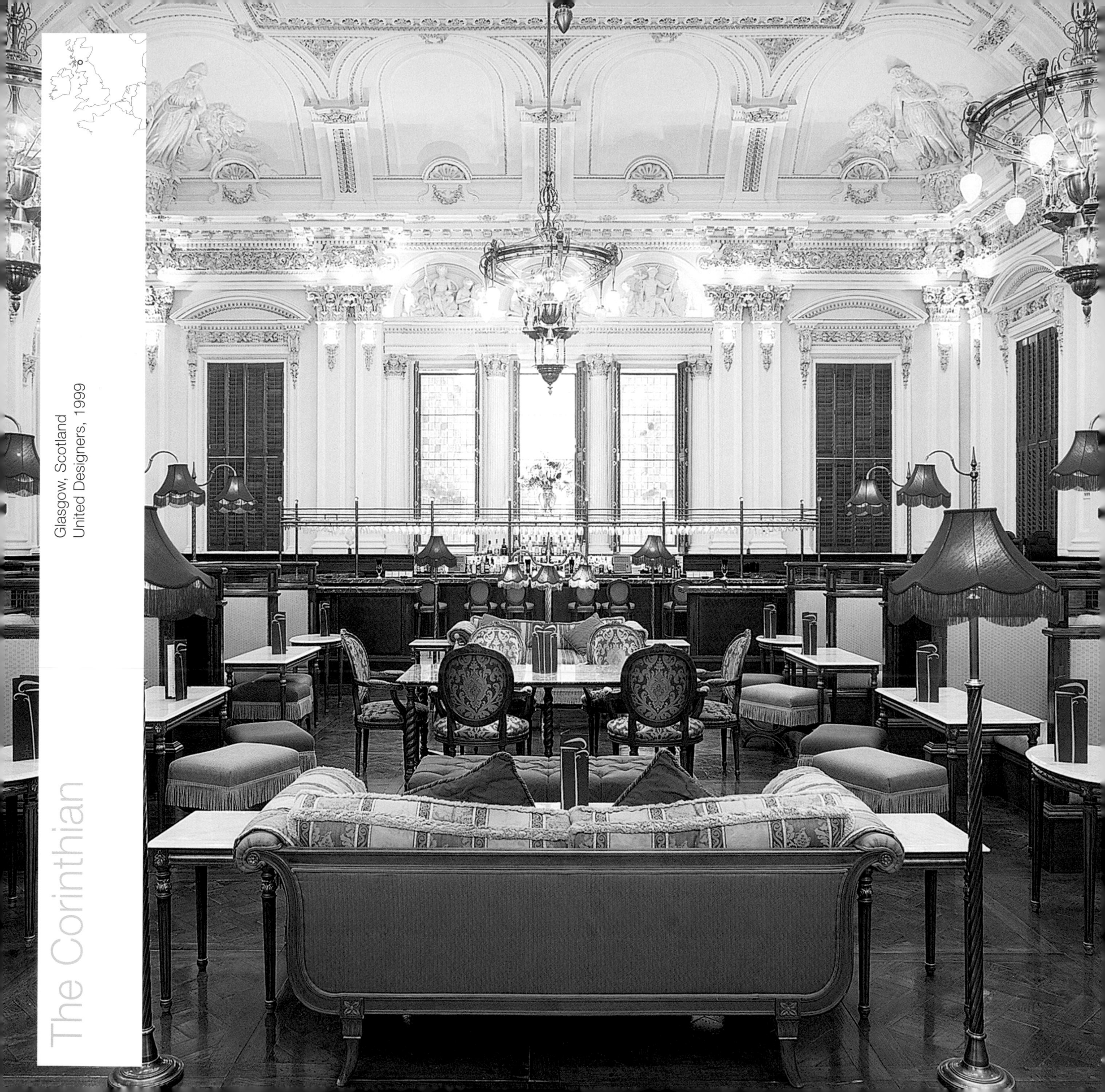

The Corinthian

Glasgow, Scotland
United Designers, 1999

Opposite:
The main bar occupies the
Telling Room of what was once
a Victorian bank. The renovation
included a faithful restoration of
the original oak booths.

Right:
The glamour of the 1930s was
recreated in the two more
intimate cocktail lounge bars,
housed in the former homes of
the Procurator Fiscal and the
Clerks of the Court.

London-based design consultancy United Designers are
renowned for their 'modern classic' design approach – a
formal aesthetic displaying simple, clean lines created by
using traditional materials such as leather, marble and
timber. The Corinthian, completed in 1999 and located in
the rapidly developing Merchant City area of Glasgow, is
a stunning demonstration of their ability to both restore
and contemporize a 19th-century interior. It is also
representative of a national trend – the merging of finance
companies and centralization of banking systems has left
many fomer bank or financial buildings empty and
redundant. Often Victorian, these spacious properties
are being converted into restaurants and bars.

Originally known as Lanarkshire House, the Grade A-listed
building was built in 1852 by David Hamilton to house
the Glasgow Ship Bank and, later, the Union Bank of
Scotland. Already a landmark Victorian property, it was
remodelled by James Burnett in 1876 and over the next
30 years, highly respected architects and artists added
various classical sculptures and features, including the
spectacular 8 metre (26 foot) glass dome, constructed
by James Salmon. In 1929 the interior was divided up
to accommodate the city's High Court and many of the
original Victorian features, including the dome and intricate
cornices, were concealed by false partitions and ceilings.
Phase one of the transformation from derelict shell to the
Corinthian, a multi-purpose leisure and business venue,
began in 1998.

All fake and extraneous elements were removed and
considerable restoration work was undertaken.
Architectural historian George Fairful Smith uncovered an
1855 photograph of the Telling Room, now the Main Bar,
and this was used as a reference to recreate the
splendour of the original features. Gold-leaf detailing on
the walls was painstakingly restored, exquisite chandeliers,
each weighing $4\frac{1}{2}$ tonnes, were recreated in Italy and the
four cornice figurines, representing Europe, Asia, America
and Africa – Scotland's trading partners during the days
of the British Empire – were reconstructed.

Below this magnificent ceiling, with its intricate glass
crown, United Designers recreated the oak telling booths,
which now serve as intimate drinking and dining areas in
the new Corinthian. The oak panelling and parquet flooring
were new additions, although they are in keeping with the
original character of the interior. Although there is an
abundance of natural light in the Main Bar, a complex
lighting system was devised to allow an element of
flexibility. Concealed and individually dimmable neon white
and blue lights, set at a low wattage, were staggered at
three levels leading up to the dome. The blue neon is used
at night, casting a calm, atmospheric hue over the Main
Bar and setting the dome strangely aglow from outside.

In addition to the Main Bar, two smaller bars – the Cocktail
Bar and the Piano Bar – were created in the former
homes of the Procurator Fiscal and the Clerks of the
Court. Rich, luxurious materials and colours were chosen

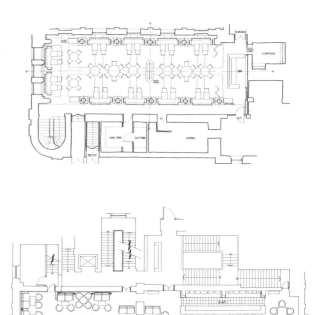

to exude the glamour of the 1930s. The full-height
windows, which overlook the Glasgow streets, have been
draped in green-gold silk drapes to allow drinkers to hide
away and imbibe. Comfort is foremost – sofas, tub chairs
and the bar front have been upholstered in oxblood-red
leather and the oversized standard lamps keep lighting
soft and low. The contemporary lines of the furnishings
and details, such as the recessed lighting set behind huge
diamond-cut mirrors, angled to reflect and enlarge the
space, lend a modern edge to the classic backdrop of
oak panelling, parquet flooring and deep, rich colours
and materials.

Phase two includes a dining restaurant adjacent to the
Main Bar on the ground floor, two basement nightclubs –
Life and Q – in the former jail cells, and on the upper
levels a private dining room, private members' bar,
conference facilities and corporate board room. The
Corinthian is aimed at professional 'thirtysomethings'
and open until the early hours of the morning seven days
a week. As United Designers say, 'Whether you're dining,
dancing, drinking or debriefing, the Corinthian has all you
need underneath one splendid domed roof.'

Plans:
Ground-floor plans of the
restaurant (top) and the private
members' bar (above). There are
additional leisure and corporate
business facilities in the basement
and upper levels.

Right:
The spectacular 8 metre (26 foot)
glass dome, originally constructed
by James Salmon in the 19th
century, is the Corinthian's
crowning glory.

Soft

Main image left:
The furniture is arranged in a stark, white interior, like artworks exhibited in a contemporary art gallery, endowing Soft with a surreal character.

Right:
When is a bar stool not a bar stool? When it's custom-designed by Airconditioned and is a chair fixed to the top of a white stool.

Although design group Airconditioned describe Soft as a 'contemporary British pub', the former karaoke bar is more redolent of a modern art installation. Funky furniture is arranged against the stark, white interior walls of this small basement bar, like artworks exhibited in an archetypal white-cube gallery. Soft is full of trickery – there is a humour in the design that is comparable to interiors by the great master of illusion, Philippe Starck, with visual puns on proportion and, of course, a quirky toilet feature.

The entrance and stairway down to the bar are shrouded in darkness until people arrive and then the sensor-activated lights come on. Inside, a high, white counter poses as the bar – with no bottles visible so as not to interfere with the clean, white backdrop. Barflies have to clamber up onto bar stools that appear like chairs floating in mid-air. Custom-designed for the project, there is a touch of surreal, Magritte magic in these creations. When is a bar stool not a bar stool – evidently when it's by Airconditioned and it's a chair balanced on top of another stool. As Airconditioned member Hitoshi Saeki has said in interview (*Frame*, no.17, 2000), 'We design human activity. It's not always a smooth ride, but it's a lot of fun.'

It is the furniture throughout that endows Soft with its unusual character. Adjacent to the bar is a row of white tables and chairs by El Ultimo Grito, all very much in keeping with the white-on-white theme, with simple steel stands and acrylic white tops. In the opposite corner, a group of bespoke chairs by Jam are gathered around four

small white squares, suspended by white rods from the ceiling, literally turning the concept of table on its head. MEMO sofas by Inflate are also strewn around, adding colour and providing flexible, more casual seating. Tables are lit by candles and downlighting, and an orange fluorescent uplight adds warmth to the bar area.

Those guests visually literate enough in the language of modern design to find the toilet (through a door in the wall with no handle) will find themselves in another riddle of a space. Again, the light is sensor-activated, coming on when visitors enter. They find themselves in a glowing orange cubicle, where the toilet roll is positioned so high it requires forward planning and the tap releases a column of water from the ceiling. Soft may well be a contemporary British pub, but most definitely not one as we know it.

Above:
The glowing orange toilet cubicle is a riddle of a space, located behind a door with no handle. The position of the toilet roll requires forward planning.

Main image right:
Bespoke chairs by JAM surround small white squares that are suspended from the ceiling by rods. The concept of 'table' is literally turned on its head.

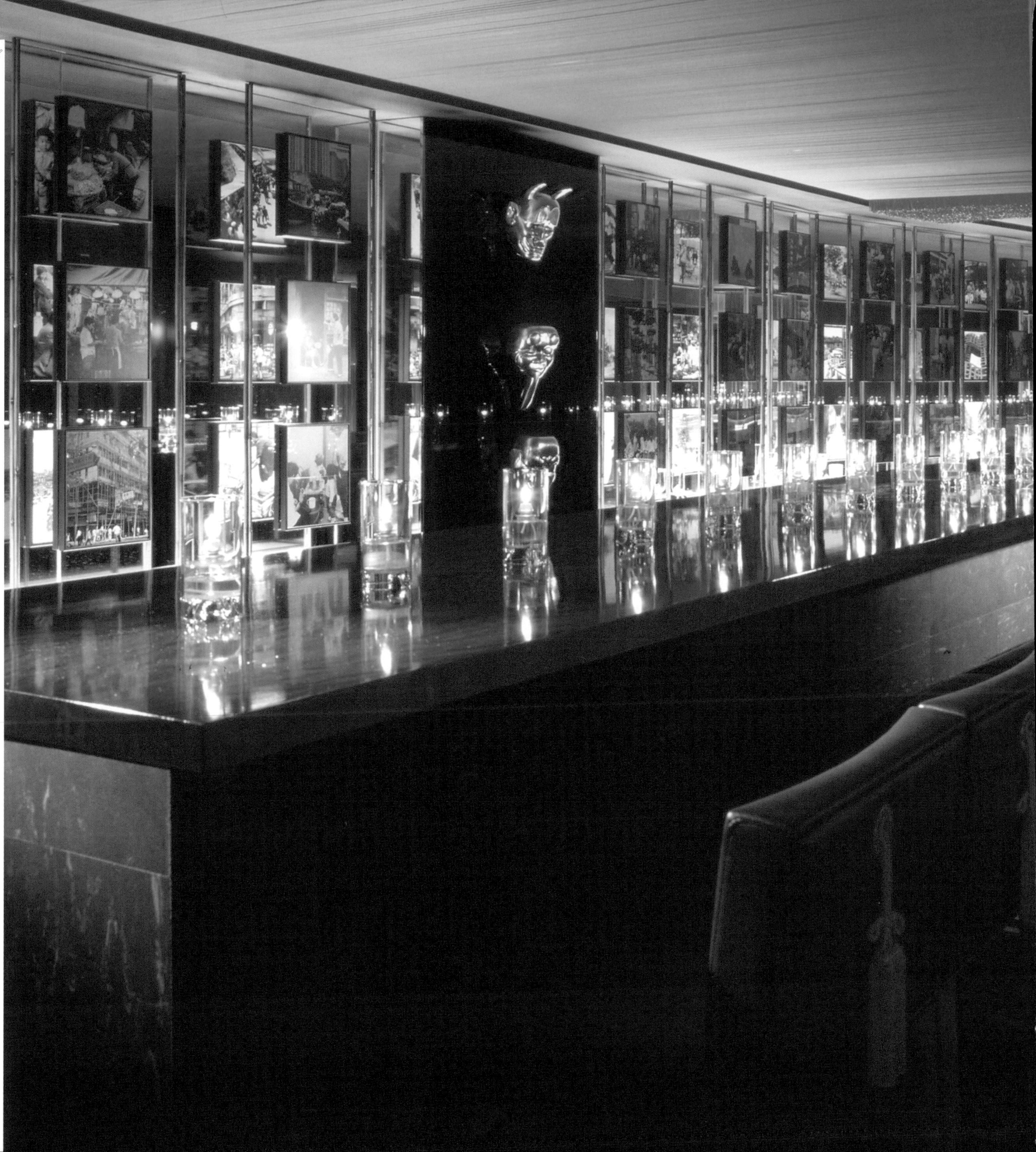

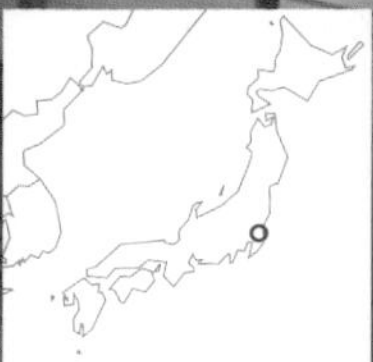

BAR Ballad BAR

Tokyo, Japan
Yasumichi Morita, 1999

Designer Yasumichi Morita describes the interior as a 'tense balance between stylish modernity and traditional reminiscence'.

Opposite:
Silver masks from Noh theatre –
a traditional Japanese dramatic
genre – line the entrance corridor.

Right and far right:
The sensual red vinyl ceiling is
counter-balanced by the warmth
of the glossy cherrywood bar
counter below.

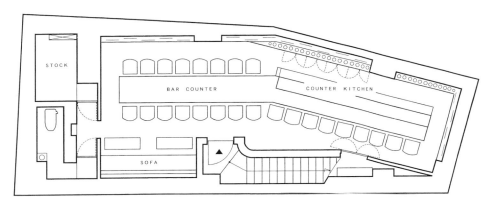

STOCK

BAR COUNTER   COUNTER KITCHEN

SOFA

Plan:
The long table consists of two
halves, which are joined at an
angle to compensate for the
awkward shape of the room. One
half operates as a communal
table seating 16 guests, the other
as a conventional bar counter.

Yasumichi Morita collaborated with several Japanese
design luminaries to produce this chic little bar (31 person
capacity) in Tokyo's Aoyama district, known for its
designer furniture shops. Yasuo Kondo created the ceiling
and wall lined with red vinyl ropes, while interior designer
Takashi Sugimoto was responsible for the Japanese
cherrywood top of the long, central table and the bar
counter. Photographer Takao Kitayma contributed the
images of Japan, Vietnam, China and the Philippines
from the 1950s–80s. Morita took care of the details and
oversaw the project, which he feels contains 'a tense
balance between stylish modernity and traditional
reminiscence'.

The Japanese character of the bar is created by the
'folk material' details – Morita has framed Kitayma's
photographs in bamboo and lined them along the uplit
mirrored wall. On the reverse of each picture is another
photograph, this second image reflected in the mirror.
The result is an illusion of depth and is Morita's way of
creating scenery for the client, who would have loved
window views had the bar not been below ground.

The silver masks on display come from Noh theatre –
a traditional Japanese dramatic genre. Originally these
would have been made of wood but Morita has added a
contemporary twist by designing chrome-plated versions.
A further theatrical reference can be found in the red
tassel detail on the back of each chair. Lighting is
subdued but focused; aside from the uplit mirrored wall,

there are 40 miniature oil lamps spaced 20 centimetres (8
inches) apart along the central counter. These highlight the
texture and red dye of the cherrywood counter top, which
provides a tonal balance to the warmth of the vinyl ceiling.

Hotel bars

Bar Tempo/Claridge's Bar/Crowne Plaza Bar/Absolut Icebar/
Time (Interga___ic) Beach E___Miramar Hotel E___Purple E
Hotel Atoll Bar/Dietrich's/Mink Bar/Hudson Hotel Bar/
Mandarin Bar/The Church Lounge

Bar Tempo
Mojiko Hotel

Kitakyushu, Japan
Shigeru Uchida, 1998

The cherrywood bar counter is
positioned along the windows to
offer panoramic views of the
Kanmon Straits.

Travellers seeking comfort and respite would not be
disappointed by Bar Tempo, situated on the top floor
of the 'hotel by the sea', the Mojiko Hotel in Japan. The
L-shaped space, with its deep-red interior and luxurious
finishes, exudes warmth, from the cherrywood of the
ceiling and bar counter to the fully operative antique
fireplace in the lounge area. The entire hotel scheme is
the product of a collaboration between the famous, late
Italian architect Aldo Rossi and interior architect Shigeru
Uchida. It is situated on a piece of land protruding into
Moji harbour.

The owners' request that the bar afford views of the
Kanmon Straits has been dramatically fulfilled by the
positioning of the bar counter along the length of the
window wall. Guests seated at the bar are privy to a
panoramic view of the inlet – an expanse of water with
the twinkling lights of the opposite shore in the distance.
This area is ideal for single guests or couples, whereas
the slightly sunken lounge area tucked around the
corner, furnished with sofas and club chairs, is more
accommodating for group parties. The blue-green roof
of the neo-Renaissance-styled Mojiko Station is visible
from the lounge windows.

Entertainment is provided by a grand piano, placed in
the centre of the room to ensure that all the guests
are able to enjoy the live music. The deep green and
charcoal tones of the suede furniture upholstery provide
a tonal balance with the red wall tiles. Classically styled

Main image right:
The deep-red interior exudes
warmth, from the classically
styled wall tiles to the fully
operative antique fireplace.

Plan:
The grand piano has been placed
in the corner of the L-shaped
interior to ensure that guests
at the long bar counter and in
the lounge area can enjoy the
live music.

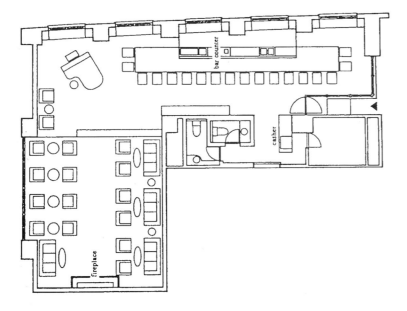

and especially indicative of Japanese design, these tiles
were chosen to blend with the historical image of the area.
Apart from down-lighting, which is positioned over seated
areas and within each window, ambient light is generated
by occasional bespoke floor lamps, each one forming an
integrated motif of the Mojiko Hotel.

Uchida is a strong believer in architecture either
confronting or assimilating the pervading spirit of a place.
The strong but simple design of Bar Tempo must be
understood in the context of the hotel as a whole.
Uchida describes the Mojiko Hotel in the following way:
'The architectural interior derives its form from the cultural
elements that are rooted in the region, these elements
being surprisingly tenacious and resistant to the times
or the influence of another culture.'

London, UK
David Collins, 1998

Claridge's Bar
Claridge's Hotel

Main image left:
Stately and elegant, the new bar, created in collaboration with English Heritage, exudes an old-fashioned, Edwardian air, befitting its host hotel.

Right:
Luxurious materials include walls that are padded with green silk in the snug and bespoke raw-silk curtains, downlit to appear like abstract artworks.

Claridge's Bar may be small, but what it lacks in size it makes up for in glamour. David Collins designed the bar in collaboration with the British governmental agency English Heritage, to ensure that the interior was in keeping with the listed art deco hotel interior. The creation of a new bar at Claridge's, accessible from the lobby but also with its own separate street entrance, should be considered in the wider context of the 'Schragerization' of hotel bars – the trend pioneered by hotelier Ian Schrager to revive hotel bars and to make them as attractive to the 'indigenous' population as to visiting hotel residents. Although Collins's design is classic and traditional, unlike the quirky, über-hip hotel bars designed by Philippe Starck, it has still proved extremely popular with London's fashionistas.

Previously the Causerie, the new interior exudes a stately elegance befitting its host hotel and its Mayfair location. The muted silver and eau-de-Nil colour scheme and classic materials, such as walnut parquet flooring and the onyx bar counter, crackled in appearance like old bone china, convey a sense of luxury. It is a relaxed space – definitely no standing up. Guests can opt for the chunky, circular bar stools, upholstered in deep-red leather or red, mock-crocodile leather, or for sofas and chairs.

The fireplace provides the main room with a warm heart. Set into a wall, it separates the main bar from the smaller snug. This cosy enclosure, tucked behind the fireplace, is quieter and more private, with the padded green silk ceiling and walls blocking out sound. Aside from the objet-trouvé chandelier in the main bar, all lighting, including the perspex hexagonal lights, was custom-designed by Collins for the project. It is the bespoke raw-silk curtains that truly complete the scene – drawn after dark and then downlit, they appear like abstract works of art, adding splashes of colour to the room.

New York City, USA
Adam Tihany, 2000

Crowne Plaza Bar
Crowne Plaza New York

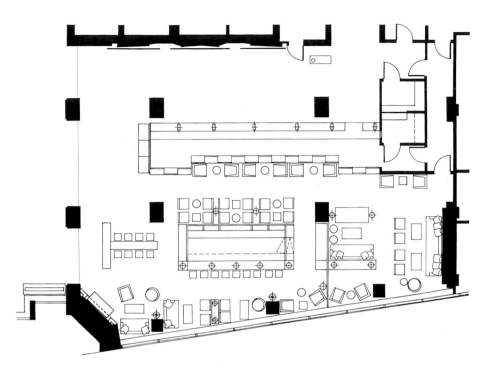

Plan:
The hotel bar consists of a main bar room and adjoining lounge, with areas divided off by stainless-steel and frosted glass panels.

Above right:
Large-scale, abstract forms represent trees. Rosewood columns and glass panels suggest the angular growth of a tree trunk.

Left:
As the bar's central design motif, the tree has been incorporated in various ways, from images of forests presented on hi-tech LCD screens to rough, bark-covered logs, masquerading as art installations.

Adam Tihany's recent refurbishment of the bar at New York's Crowne Plaza Hotel mixes sleek, modern finishes with organic, natural forms. Tihany chose 'the tree' as the central design motif, to represent growing concern for the environment at the turn of the millennium, but this is presented with up-to-date technology, such as small LCD screens, embedded in sawdust, displaying images of trees and forests. Large-scale, iconographic abstractions of trees capture the imagination of guests, such as the rosewood columns that appear like bold, Cubist-style trunks, sprouting through the ceiling.

Similarly, the dividing wall that separates the lounge area from the access corridor is constructed from frosted glass and stainless-steel panels. These are angled alternately to suggest the growth of a tree trunk. Each one is uplit to provide a glamorous, diffuse light. More obvious timber features are the rough, bark-covered logs suspended from the ceiling, positioned to connect each of the square light boxes. Tihany has also made the tree into an art installation by placing a 2.5 metre (8 foot) long log in a glass display case.

A dozen people can sit at the bar, on custom-made mahogany stools, with tan leather-covered seats. The lounge, furnished with bespoke sofas and club chairs, accommodates a further 30 guests. The stainless-steel-framed furniture displays modern, clean lines whilst the dark-brown leather upholstery and red and tan mohair seats and cushions provide the comfort. The natural

richness of wood is evident in practical aspects of the bar as well, such as the dark ebony table tops, and the rich Brazilian cherrywood floor. Bespoke lamps add warmth and bright yellow splashes of colour contrast with the cold blues of the frosted glass. By night, the natural flicker of table candlelight sets a more intimate tone.

Jukkasjärvi, Sweden

Åke Larsson and Arne Bergh, 2000

Absolut Icebar

Icehotel 2000–1

Main image left:
Every November crystal-clear ice is cut from the River Torne to create the translucent, winter-wonderland interiors of the Icehotel and Icebar.

Above:
The bar occupies a dome that is 10 metres (33 feet) high. Once completed, a gallery and restaurant will also be opened.

Not many bars are rebuilt every year, but then not many are constructed in ice. The Absolut Icebar has been recreated annually since 1989 as part of the Icehotel, located in Jukkasjärvi, 200 kilometres (124 miles) north of the Artic Circle in Swedish Lapland. Construction begins in early November, with the main structure complete by December and interior work continuing into January. Åke Larsson and Arne Bergh design the Icehotel every year and, although the bar is sponsored by Absolut vodka, are given the freedom to integrate the brand into their design however they wish.

The Icehotel 2000–1 is formed from crystal-clear ice cut from the River Torne with special tools custom-made in Jukkasjärvi. Snow canons and front loaders are used to mould dense snow, called 'snice', over huge, vaulted steel forms. After two days, these vaulted sections are moved to the chosen location and the ice support columns are then inserted inside. Next, international artists and sculptors concentrate on creating the architectural details and sculptures from ice blocks that transform the interior into a hotel-cum-transient art piece, which melts away in April. Previous Absolut Icebar designs have included ice-screens for showing videos, doorways in the shape of enormous Absolut bottles and a 'barhanger' – a full-size iceman sculpture, leaning on the bar counter.

The Absolut Icebar is situated at the end of a 40 metre (131 foot) hallway, flanked by ice columns and containing sculpture and furniture, and is strewn with thick reindeer

Left:
Blood-red vodka cocktails, containing the juices of local fruits, are served up in shot glasses formed from blocks of ice.

Far left:
The designers are given the freedom to integrate the Absolut Vodka brand into their design however they wish. In a previous Icehotel, doorways were cut in the shape of the iconic bottle.

Plan:
The Absolut Icebar 2000–1 consists of a long hallway, flanked by columns, and containing sculpture and furniture, which leads up to a spectacular dome area that houses the actual bar.

Main image right:
International artists and sculptors create the architectural details and ornately carved furniture, transforming the interior into a bar-cum-transient art piece.

skins for comfort and warmth. The hall leads up to a spectacular ice dome containing the bar and measuring 14 metres (46 feet) in diameter and 10 metres (33 feet) in height. The ice wall on the opposite side of the dome will eventually lead through into an ice gallery and restaurant. Larsson and Bergh have incorporated Absolut branding by carving giant vodka bottle reliefs from ice and snow into the wall behind the bar, which are spotlit like artworks. Colour in this icy, translucent environment is created by the changing natural light outside and by candles inside, which warm up the cold, blue interior with their orange glow. In addition, vodka cocktails, containing local fruits such as cloudberry and lingonberry and served in clear, ice-cube glasses, add further splashes of colour to this igloo-inspired work of art.

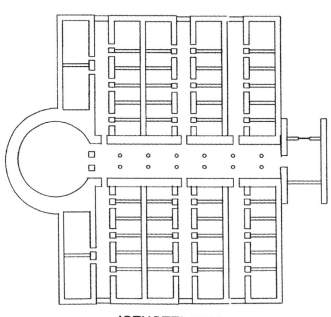

ICEHOTEL 2001

Whitley Bay, UK
Paul Daly, 1998

Time (Intergalactic)
Beach Bar

Time (Intergalactic) Beach Bar is full of curvaceous, retro-futuro shapes and fluid lines. Daly's bespoke 'Yoga' beer fonts rise up like swans' necks from the bar counter and, above, Jeremy Lord's 'Chromawall' light installation flashes different colours like the landing lights of some spacecraft.

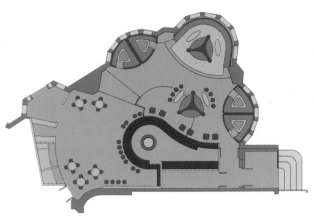

The funky, futuristic furniture, 1970s colours and spacey forms of the Time (Intergalactic) Beach Bar make it unmistakably Daly. The London-based designer Paul Daly is fine-art-trained and first began applying the skills he practised as a sculptor to create furniture and products in the early 1990s. He now concentrates on constructing whole interiors. Daly specializes in bars and restaurants – for the Time (Intergalactic) Beach Bar, he was asked to create 'a disco 1970s-style thing' on the site of an old ballroom adjoining a hotel. The original interior was stripped out and a bay window was removed to accommodate the new entrance.

The interior is full of curvaceous shapes and fluid lines, ranging from the poured, factory-floor finish in various shades of blue, inspired by the work of the Italian designer Gaetano Pesce, to the round, flying-saucer-like extractor fans. The first thing visitors encounter on arrival is the large circular bar, featuring Daly's bespoke curved, 'Yoga' beer fonts, which rise up like graceful swans' necks from the bar counter. To the left of the entrance a raised section, with light, timber flooring forms the lounge area where three bay windows have each been furnished with blue leather banquettes to create booths.

Three pieces of furniture were custom made for the Time (Intergalactic) Beach Bar – the plywood-and-brown-leather dining and bar chairs, known respectively as 'Ply-Me-Down' and 'Ply-Me-Up', and the cheekily titled 'Ménage à Trois', a brown leather upholstered seating unit that is really three benches in one. Two of these units are positioned in the lounge area. To complete the sci-fi look, Daly collaborated with lighting innovator Jeremy Lord and created a large circular incision in the ceiling to frame Lord's 'Chromawall' light installation, which contains different coloured light squares, like the landing lights of some outer space aircraft about to touch down in Whitley Bay.

Above:
Furniture was custom-made
for the project – there are two
of these cheekily titled 'Menage
à Trois' (that's three benches
in one).

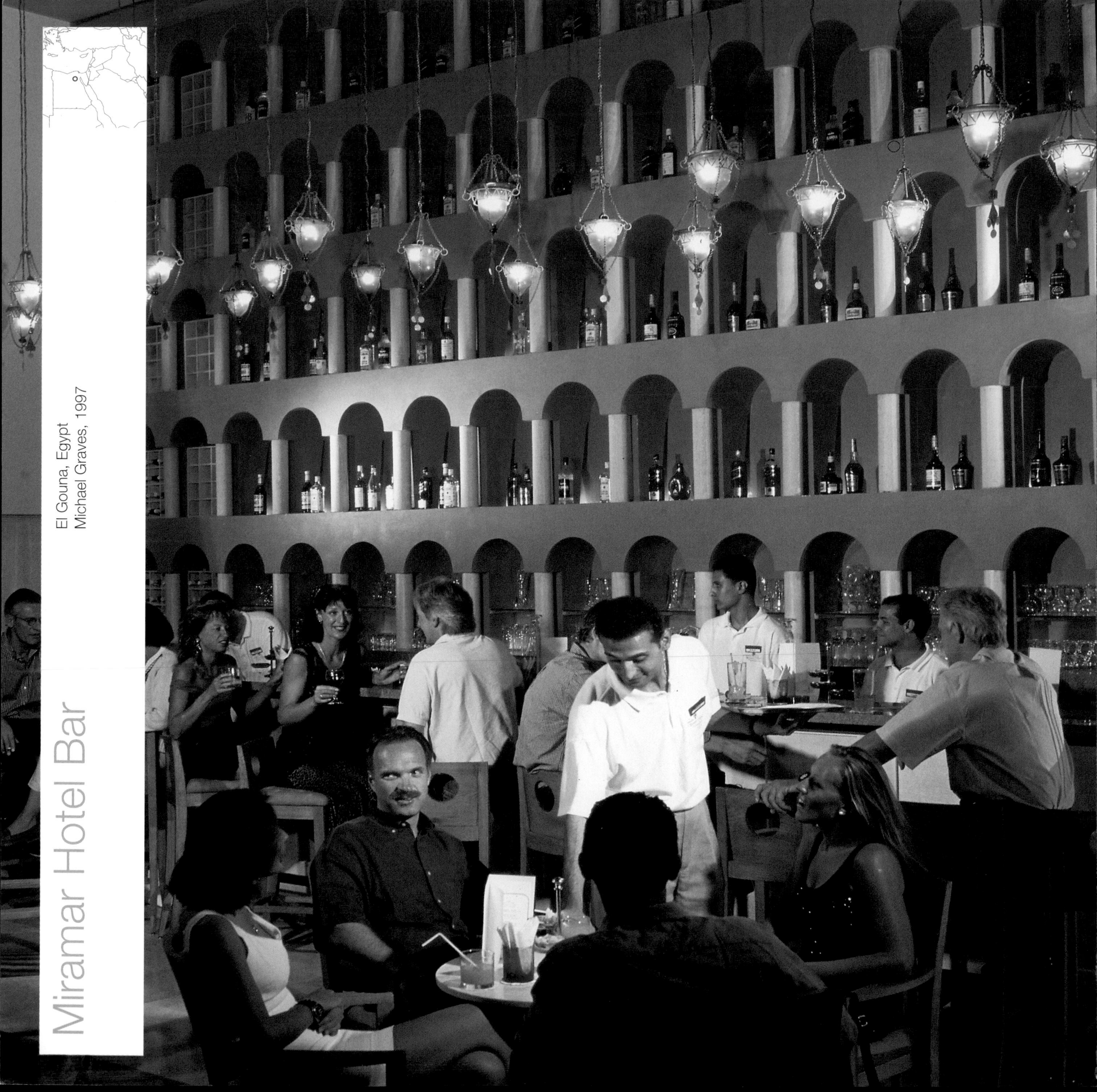

Miramar Hotel Bar

El Gouna, Egypt
Michael Graves, 1997

Opposite:
The main focus of the venue is
the back bar – level upon level of
orange niches, each one lit to
emphasize its form and the
bottles it contains.

Right:
The blue glass lamps, suspended
by chains, like religious icon
holders, were crafted locally, like
most of the project details.

Below:
The bar replicates the vernacular
Islamic forms of its host hotel.

The beauty of this hotel bar lies in the repetition of its orange niches, lit to emphasize the arches and bottles on display, and in the tension between such a grand architectural gesture and the narrow space it inhabits. The bar is framed within a single, giant arch at the centre of an elongated room. The opposite wall is lined with French windows, overlooking a terrace and the turquoise Red Sea beyond. It is very much in keeping with its host hotel, the five-star Sheraton Miramar, created by Michael Graves & Associates at the Egyptian resort of El Gouna.

The entire project covers 200,000 square metres (2,153,000 square feet) and consists of clusters of buildings arranged around landscaped gardens and man-made lagoons and pools, so that every one of the 330 guestrooms has a water view. What makes the Miramar Hotel unique is Graves's modern interpretation of vernacular architecture and his faithful application of indigenous building techniques and materials, resulting in a spectacular geometrical array of colourful domes, arches and ovals surrounded by the Red Sea. The bar replicates these forms and Islamic shapes on a smaller scale – the layers of arches that make up the back bar are the main focus; the supporting columns have been gilded for effect. The result is the Miramar in miniature.

The blue glass lamps suspended in chains, like religious icon holders, shine forth in contrast to the orange glow. They were designed by Graves but, like most of the project, crafted locally. The simple cherrywood bar stools and chairs feature circular cut-outs, which echo the holes punched in the external hotel structure and the circular apertures, or skylights, set into the domes and vaulted roofs of the guestrooms. The armchairs are upholstered in silk and cotton textiles, some with golden Pharaonic stars woven into the cloth. The bar is used mostly for post-prandial relaxation, with hotel guests spilling out onto the terrace on balmier Arabian nights.

Opposite:
The bar is an intimate, inner sanctum, all wrapped up in purple hues. Delicate detailing contrasts starkly with the rock bar face.

Above left:
Design sketches show the etched Venetian mirrorwork framing the bar's entrance.

Above right:
The Purple Bar is the perfect antidote to the hotel's showy Long Bar, which has a 24 metre (79 foot) glowing, onyx island bar.

Encased in Venetian etched glass and purple silk, this chic, regal little bar is tucked inside the lobby of Ian Schrager's Sanderson Hotel in London. The dark, candle-lit interior is in stark contrast to the rest of the public areas, which brightly showcase Philippe Starck's surreal, theatrical aesthetic that has made Schrager's London hotels so unique. Schrager pioneered the 'boutique' concept back in the 1980s with Morgan's Hotel in Manhattan, New York. His aim was to revitalize hotels, awaken people to 'lobby living' and transform hotels into the 'nightclubs of the 90s'. Unsurprising really, given that this is the man who, along with business partner the late Steve Rubell, created possibly the most notorious, celebrated star-studded club of all time, the legendary Studio 54.

Now Schrager, 'hip hotelier', has a host of places where the world's glitterati, style- and star-conscious rest and play. The hotel bars are the hotspots, destinations where the city's movers and shakers can mix with more cosmopolitan guests. Indeed, these hotel bars are so successful that it has become necessary to provide several bars in one property – an accessible main bar and a smaller, often more exclusive bar. At the Sanderson the Purple Bar is an antidote to the Long Bar – a 24 metre (80 foot) glowing onyx island bar that is usually buzzing and surrounded by people perching on the white bar stools. Purple is the intimate, inner sanctum for residents and VIPs only, and seats no more than 40 guests.

All wrapped up in purple hues, with plush velvet banquettes, silk opera drapes lining the walls and a ceiling padded in buttoned silk, the Purple Bar is soundproofed, calm and subdued. It has features that allude to Alice in Wonderland, such as miniature Queen Anne chairs, small, bespoke African wooden stools and, of course, the mirrorwork. Are we stepping through the looking glass? The Venetian etched glass is a recurring design motif in the Sanderson and has been used throughout the bar, from the lavender mirrored glass doorway to the circular table tops and the framing around the bar. Such delicate, palatial details are thrown into relief against the centrepiece – the rock face of the bar – formed from uncut Nero Apsoluto stone and dramatically spotlit for full effect. Lighting is focused on the bar and back shelves stocked with a panoply of vodkas. The rest of the room fades away into purple oblivion and flickering candlelight.

Hotel Atoll Bar

Heligoland, Germany
Alison Brooks Architects, 1999

Above:
Arne Jacobsen's Swan chairs
occupy an area just beyond the
bar's gravitational pull.

Left:
The bar is formed from an
aluminium cylinder that appears
to have been sliced open
diagonally, forming what the
designer, Alison Brooks,
describes as an 'inner void', lit
by the illuminated lid above.

The lobby bar of the Hotel Atoll, on the remote German island of Heligoland in the North Sea, is a conceptual microcosm of the rest of this spa hotel. It was a man-made atoll, a floating, steel diving platform off the coast of Heligoland, saved from extinction by Hamburg industrialist Arne Weber, that provided the hotel's name and the inspiration for architect Alison Brooks, creator of the hotel's interiors. The circular bar is constructed from an aluminium cylinder that appears to have been sliced open diagonally to create an internally illuminated 'lid', hanging above what Brooks describes as an 'inner void', in which the bartender is housed. Evocative of something from outer space, in the context of Hotel Atoll it is redolent of some kind of sea creature, like a giant clam.

The entire scheme plays on aquatic forms. In the hotel foyer, for example, the sea-green terrazzo floor has been punctuated by large, stainless-steel cones, which provide an aerial view of swimmers in the hotel pool below. Elsewhere, the glass pod-enclosed bistro features a communal dining table in the centre that is shaped like a starfish or coral fauna, and a life-ring-shaped object that resembles a jellyfish houses the female toilets. The architectural plans clearly display the fluid, circular geometry favoured by Brooks that can be seen in the bar, foyer, bistro, shop and glass seating booths in the restaurant – all arranged within an L-shaped space.

Above:
Glass-backed seating allows
light to flood into the restaurant.

Sketch:
Tall, convex copper panels,
redolent of vertebrae, encircle
the bar, separating it from the
lobby space.

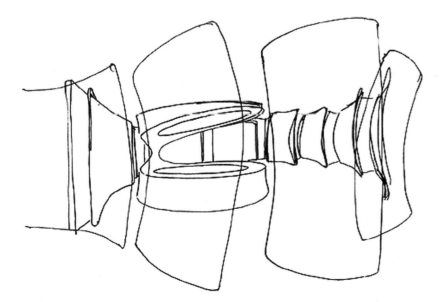

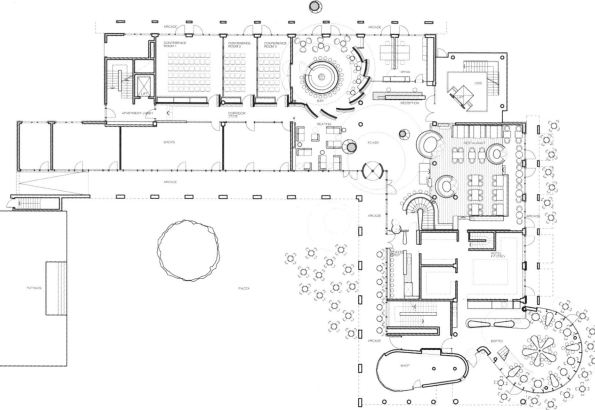

Above:
Guests in the lobby, thanks to the large 'viewing' cones that punctuate the sea-green terrazzo floor, can spy on swimmers below.

Plan:
The fluid, almost organic geometry favoured by Brooks is evident in the bar, shop and bistro, and throughout the L-shaped space.

Opposite:
The panels surrounding the bar fan outwards, echoing the form and movement of a sea anemone.

Shimmering, convex copper panels encircle the bar, separating it from the lobby. They are a continuation of the concave copper wall, which encloses the adjoining conference rooms. Brooks says the copper wall originated from the desire to 'make a corridor breathe and express wave-like motion'. This was then extended to form an enclosure around the bar that could open and close depending on its use. However, the impracticality of fabricating copper panels with double curvature led to Brooks 'fragmenting and overlapping segments of the wall, which began to appear like scales, or vertebrae, coiling around the bar'.

The panels' 'unfixed' appearance adds to the sense of movement already conveyed by the dynamic, 'open' nature of the bar. Indeed, even when empty, the bar appears animated, surrounded as it is by Bombo stools by Magis, reminiscent of floating wisps of jellyfish or UFOs. Curvaceous Swan chairs by Arne Jacobsen occupy the area just outside the bar's gravitational pull, creating a small lounge by the windows. There is a strong, futuristic element to the design, but it's less space-age and more 'sea odyssey 2001'. And there may be more to come – it is Weber's ambition eventually to transform the atoll itself into a floating bar.

Dietrich's
Grand Hyatt Berlin

Berlin, Germany
Dani Freixas & Varis Architects, 2000

Opposite:
Small lamps, made of white opalescent glass and fixed to the centre of the counter tops, send out a soft glow by night.

Right:
The glowing wall is formed from 'sandwiches' of red cedarwood, yellow oak laminate and glass, retro-lit by a fluorescent light and suspended from a stainless-steel structure. A fan of solid wooden slats, hung from the ceiling, conceals the air conditioning units.

Plan:
Guests can sit one side of the zigzag bar counter, face-to-face on either side of the two communal tables or in the round on the circular tables for six.

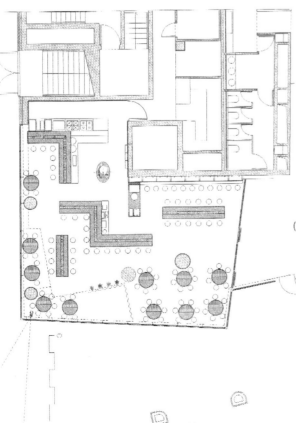

It seems fitting that the bar counter at Dietrich's is fragmented, consisting of several zig-zag pieces, since the venue is located in an area close to where the Berlin Wall once stood. Since the fall of the Berlin Wall, this district has developed rapidly, becoming an important business and leisure area, with cinemas, bars and clubs. Dietrich's is on the ground floor of the new Grand Hyatt Hotel, overlooking Marlene-Dietrich-Platz, and although it was intended originally to be a noodle bar, and later a Russian restaurant, it has ended up as a beer and fast food bar.

Inside, the illuminated, panelled wall is the bar's most distinctive element and is recognizable as the work of Dani Freixas. Freixas is fascinated by light, as he has said in interview (*Frame*, no. 9, 1999): 'I love its immaterial nature, its expansive form, its ability to colour spaces, its flexibility in defining outlines. I use it to create shadows, to establish hierarchies, and to qualify the perception of architectural elements or routes that cut through the space.' In Dietrich's, the backlit panelling functions like a giant vertical lamp, emitting a gentle, diffuse kind of light. Visible from the exterior, it sends out an attractive glow, making the bar appealing to the passer-by.

The glowing panels are formed from 'sandwiches' of wood laminate and glass, which are retro-lit by a fluorescent source and hung from a stainless steel structure. The combination of red cedar wood and yellow oak varies the intensity of the light. After dark, a more intimate atmosphere is created by the small table lamps.

These white, opalescent glass cylinders send out a soft, natural light, and make a visual connection between the two communal tables and the two halves of the bar counter.

Suspended from the ceiling above the bar are solid wood slats, spaced 5 centimetres (2 inches) apart and configured to form a fan-like structure of different heights. This serves to conceal the air-conditioning, but also connects the different areas of the room. Seating is provided in the form of stainless steel and natural stone-topped stools, organized around the high, circular tables and counters – not conducive to leisurely lounging, such furniture is ideal for a beer and fast food bar, where a high turnover of guests is expected. The circular tables, located around the periphery of the space, feature two-tone wooden tops, in harmony with the cedar and oak of the wall panels. Three sides of the bar are lined by windows and, in summer, guests spill out onto the porch area.

Melbourne, Australia
Wayne Finschi, 1999

Mink Bar
Prince of Wales Hotel

Above left:
One of the snug 'retreats' where the elite can find privacy behind velvet drapes.

Above right:
Russian poster imagery and propaganda decorate the interior.

Main image left:
Back in the USSR, the main bar is simple and utilitarian, with basic timber furniture and distressed plaster walls.

No modern city is complete without its very own Russian-themed vodka and caviar bar. Melbourne's Soviet-style drinking den is located in the basement of the Prince of Wales Hotel in Melbourne. Created by Wayne Finschi, the Mink Bar juxtaposes utilitarian decor in the main bar with a retro classic lounge and plush decadence in the velvet-lined booths.

As the designer explains, 'The interior architecture was intentionally simple – a stripped-down basement application. We introduced small window-niche openings, which visually connect rooms and passageways and allow discreet people viewing.' Square lamps, constructed from forged steel and glass, light each wall aperture with a warm glow. Oak parquet flooring, leather benches and simple timber chairs and tables create a richly burnished but utilitarian theme in the main bar, with authentic Russian poster imagery and propaganda adding colour to the distressed plaster walls.

The dimly lit lounge is furnished with retro leather sofas and godfather of socialism, Karl Marx, stares down from the wall. Far from the working crowd, those of an elitist persuasion can disappear into one of the 'retreats'. Regal havens of purple and red velvet, these snugs seat only a select few. One tug of a velvet cord makes them private and the flick of a button illuminates a 'Do not disturb' sign – enough to warn away the proletariat. At least until the revolution, that is.

Trip the light fantastic: Schrager's 1970s disco legacy and his urge to make hotels the nightclubs of the 1990s meets Starck's kitsch and surreal style in the design of the Hudson Hotel Bar.

The 1000-room Hudson is hotelier Ian Schrager's first Manhattan hotel in more than a decade and the bar is, true to form, proving to be a major hit with hotel residents and local New Yorkers alike. Star designer Philippe Starck is responsible for the overall design, which has been described by Schrager as 'organised chaos – a reflection and distillation of New York itself, a melting pot of styles and ideas – shimmering with hot-rod vivacity and in-your-face style'. Guests are transported from street level to the lobby and bar via a vivid chartreuse-lit, glass-encased escalator, which runs parallel to a stairway for departing guests.

The Hudson Hotel Bar is perhaps the most 'discotastic' hotel bar ever created – the floor literally lights up Saturday-Night-Fever style. It was Schrager's ambition that hotels become the nightclubs of the 1990s and this bar might even be a tribute to his Studio 54 heritage. A kitsch but chic collection of objects masquerading as furniture litters the dazzling floor, ranging from Louis XV chairs to a wooden log sprouting chair backs and a few sofas nestling in gilt brick niches set into the red brick wall. Plexiglas stools, tables that resemble oversized, clear vases, and tables and chairs with see-through plastic legs all work to create a sense of translucency. An abstract painting, depicting a phantasmagorical scene by artist Francesco Clemente enlivens the ceiling above. The long free-standing marble bar has two antique armoires behind it, which serve as the back bar. Starck's interiors are often described as surreal, a view with which he readily agrees.

In an interview with *Bare* magazine (March–April 2001), he says: 'My main tool is surrealism. It's very friendly and accessible at different levels of perception. That's why I use oversized objects and colours like ugly green – to create fertile surprise.'

The Hudson Hotel Bar is a prime example of the 'hotel as theatre' concept Schrager pioneered with Starck back in the 1980s with the Royalton Hotel. But more than this, the bar represents the idea of 'hotel bar as illuminated showcase', displaying the glamorous inhabitants who are attracted to 'boutique hotels' and who like to party, pose and parade in a venue built on the premise that 'you are where you sleep' – or drink, for that matter.

London, UK
Adam Tihany, 2000

Mandarin Bar
Mandarin Oriental London

Right:
Guests pass from the bar
through to the restaurant via
a walkway of wine.

Main image left:
The 'catwalk bar' glows beneath
a silver-leafed ceiling. Bartenders
retreat behind the glass boxes to
prepare drinks.

The recently completed bar at the Mandarin Oriental Hyde Park Hotel in London literally glows. The 'catwalk bar' basks beneath a shimmering, coffered crown of silver leaf. There is no back bar, just a simple, clear runway allowing almost 360° service. To prepare the drinks, the bartenders retreat through the door and behind the sandblasted glass boxes, which are dramatically backlit to showcase the colourful liquor selection. New York-based designer Adam Tihany was responsible for the design and refurbishment, which also includes the two restaurants Park and Foliage, the latter linked to the bar by a walkway of wine. Wine bottles are stacked on glass shelving in clear glass 'wine rooms' (one for red and one for white) that line the corridor. The rooms' glass façades are set on a diagonal axis, thus creating a funnel-like corridor that broadens out towards the restaurant.

Tihany has employed a variety of design devices in the bar to maximise space, or at least create a sense of space in what is a relatively small area. The most obvious of these are the mirrored walls, but also the beige, silk-lined panels that are set at an angle from the wall. These conceal recessed lights, which highlight the orange wall behind, sending out a rich, warm glow, but also engender an illusion of depth. Each panel has a small showcase at its centre. These contain various drink-related objects – corkscrews, vintage cocktail accessories and a bespoke martini glass designed by Tihany for Christofle Silver.

The bar, surrounded by stools with soft, toffee-coloured leather seats, is the main focus of the room. Small, backlit glass panels have been set into the dark marble counter top, echoing the square form of the wall vitrines and providing a source of gentle uplighting for those seated at the bar. The illuminated, translucent bottle storage that replaces the traditional back bar gives drink an almost iconic status. The spotlights 'backstage' have been directed at the bottles to make them appear larger than life to guests in the bar.

A small cigar divan adjoining the bar provides a more intimate area for up to ten people. Glossy Macassar ebony frames the entrance to this more subdued area, with tobacco-brown, leather-lined walls and art deco-inspired lounge chairs. The muted, autumnal palette of browns, tans and ochres, combined with the diffuse lighting and materials and finishes such as the French limestone floor, leather sofas and club chairs, create an interior of understated elegance, very much suited to its Knightsbridge location.

Left:
Lights recessed behind the angled wall panels help to create the illusion of depth.

Plan:
Lounge seating is arranged around the periphery of the space. Adjoining the bar is a small cigar divan.

Main image right:
Liquor bottles, backlit and behind translucent glass, appear iconic and larger than life.

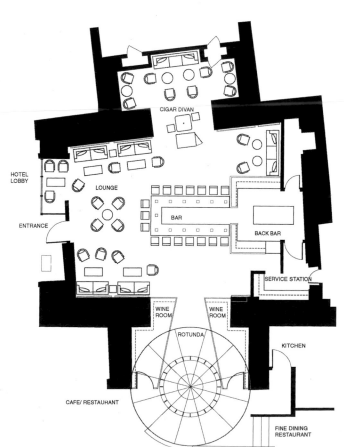

CIGAR DIVAN

HOTEL LOBBY

LOUNGE

ENTRANCE

BAR

BACK BAR

SERVICE STATION

WINE ROOM

WINE ROOM

ROTUNDA

KITCHEN

CAFE/ RESTAURANT

FINE DINING RESTAURANT

Opposite:
The triangular bar, with crimped
copper façade and sycamore
wood counter top, is at the heart
of the space.

Plan:
The triangular-formed space
houses the reception, lifts, lobby
lounge, restaurant and bar.

Far right:
Endgrain wooden pathways set
into mesquite herringbone
flooring define access routes.

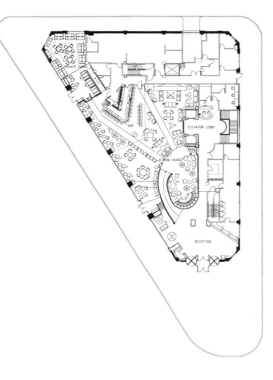

The TriBeCa Grand and its older sibling, the SoHo Grand, are both Manhattan hotels owned by father and son business partners Leonard and Emanuel Stern of Hartz Mountain Industries Inc. Their in-house architectural department designed the new hotel as an eight-storey triangular configuration, with a large central atrium that captures the very essence of TriBeCa (Triangle Below Canal Street). Bogdanow Partners Architects were enlisted to design the interior public areas.

Both clients and architects were keen to create a hotel that would be uniquely specific to TriBeCa, a place that would inspire the local community and visitors alike, becoming almost 'the town square of TriBeCa', as described by Emanuel Stern. The Sterns were keen for the design to encapsulate the 'indigenous' cast-iron architecture of the area, with its high-ceilinged interiors, copious amounts of light and graceful lines. Hence the open, atrium space with its cast-iron detailing and its skylight, 24 metres (80 feet) up, which filters light through frosted glass by day and starlight, when softly lit, by night.

Bogdanow Architects were asked to make the reception area continuous with the lobby, which would also operate as lounge, waiting room, bar, restaurant and meeting place. The space had to be fluid and flexible. Guests enter from the south corner on White Street and the 930 square metre (10,000 square foot) lobby and Church Lounge fan out before them. Access to the lounge is provided by a 3 metre (30 foot) cleft stone ramp, curving downwards around a seating area.

The Church Lounge space is well organised. Seated areas and routes are defined by Douglas fir endgrain wood, dark pathways emphasized by the surrounding mesquite herringbone flooring. There are three main seating areas preceding the bar, which is positioned towards the rear of the space. The first is enclosed by the curved ramp and another is bordered by the steel-mesh structures of the elevator cages and is organized around 'the hearth' – 66 flickering paraffin 'candles' in front of bronze tile. Measuring 7 metres (22 feet) in length and 5 metres (16 feet) in height, the hearth is framed by lacewood lintels and has patterned wood veneer panels above. The third area is tucked beneath a high alcove formed by an overhanging gallery.

Bogdanow custom-designed most of the furniture, creating small, lightweight pieces to allow flexibility. Units such as the wooden cylinders, which can be used as tables or stools, and the Victorian-style, fringed pouffes allow guests to arrange the seating to suit them. There is a variety of furniture, from café-style seating to laid-back lounge pieces, slipper chairs, sofas and loveseats upholstered in burgundy, plum, copper and blue. Table tops feature hand-painted glass designs by artist John Gerard, who also decorated the glass panels of the twin elevators. The entire west wall that runs parallel to the Avenue of the Americas is lined with red-gold crinkled-silk organza curtains, which shimmer at night, adding glamour and warmth to the space. These drapes also mysteriously thwart one's gaze from the outside looking in, although the guests inside can see out.

The triangular bar is the heart of the Church Lounge, beneath a trussed glass canopy. Its lacquered, crimped copper façade is topped with a fiddle-back sycamore wood counter, which has an ebonized ash trim. Olive-green upholstered bar stools surround the bar and line the table to the right – both bar and table feature a glowing light strip. The canopy incorporates track lighting and not only makes the space feel more intimate, but also houses a venting system that creates an 'air curtain' around the bar. Clean air is blown into the perimeter of the bar area, while smoky air is drawn into fans at its centre, behind and above the back bar, thus keeping the surrounding lounge smoke-free.

Light comes from a variety of sources. There are 70 columns of light soaring upwards, which emphasize the skylight in a dramatic fashion. Tightly beamed projection lights are anchored at the top of the atrium and set throughout the lobby. There are wall sconces, plus downlights in the soffits along the west wall, highlighting dining areas. Table candlelight throughout generates an intimate atmosphere despite the monumental scale of the space.

Clubs

B 018/The Bomb/The Supperclub/Next/Chinawhite/Jazz Matazz/
Man Ray/Bar Nil/Astro/Embassy/Lux/Zeppelin/Disco/Float/Zoom/
Café L'Atlantique/NASA/Caribou Hangar Bar

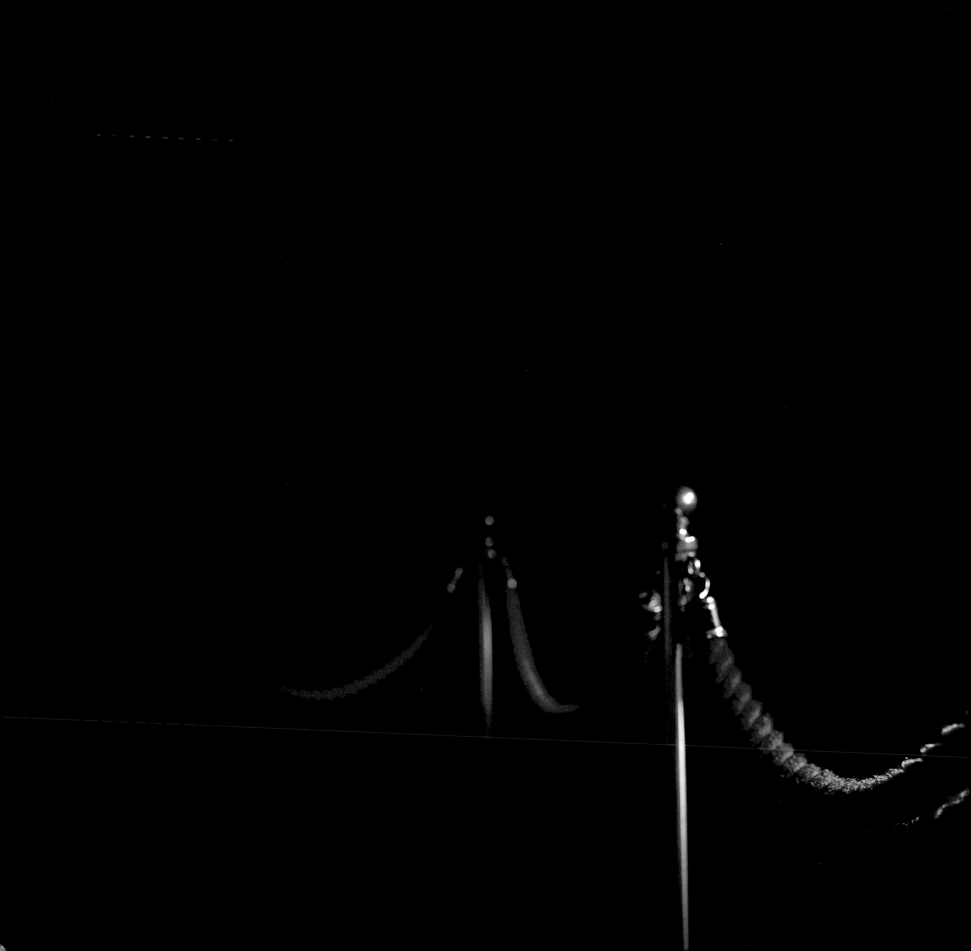

Beirut, Lebanon
Bernard Khoury, 1998

Main image left:
The subterranean bunker of a
club is bordered by a busy
motorway in the 'Rivers of Beirut'
district of the Lebanese capital.

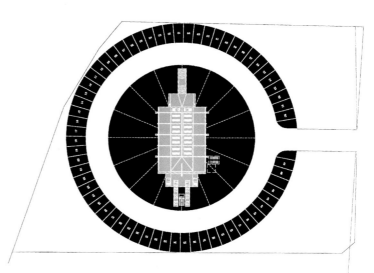

If clubbing is about escape, then it's no wonder that many of the world's most successful, most celebrated clubs are underground, offering hide-away hedonism. Yet a large number are also open-air wonderlands, offering party people the chance to dance beneath the stars. B 018 is a design masterpiece that offers both experiences. Born from the vision of architect Bernard Khoury and of musician Nagi Gebrane, this huge subterranean bunker, with its retractable roof, is sunk deep below Beirut and took six months to complete, opening in April 1998.

B 018 has a history. During Beirut's war years, Gebrane ran a club called Musical Therapy from his own apartment. It was code-named B 018 due to its location 18 kilometres (11 miles) north of the capital. It moved from obscurity to popularity between 1993 and 1997, when Gebrane went public with it, decamping to a venue in an industrial part of the Beirut suburbs. The new B 018 is in 'La Quarantaine', an area close to the port and bordered by a busy motorway and by the heavily populated 'Rivers of Beirut' district. B 018 is due to close on 8 November 2003, when the rental contract expires.

An aerial view of B 018 shows a brutish, military façade, like some giant industrial equivalent of a crop circle or a nuclear shelter embedded in concrete. The metal structure to the centre is the club's roof, which is surrounded by a ring road and parking carousel for 64 cars. Floor spotlights

Plan:
The club's retractable roof is surrounded by a ring road and parking carousel for 64 cars. By night, a circle of spotlights creates a dazzling halo of light.

divide each parking space, creating a dazzling halo
of lights around B 018 by night and conveying the
anticipatory sense that 'the spaceship has landed'.

The interior mixes functional and utilitarian design with
touches of luxury and elegance. A stairway leads to a
cavernous hall, with walls panelled in dark stained
mahogany and theatrical red curtains. The raised altar
at one end is the bar, guarded by ten fixed, pivoting
bar stools with high, sculpted backs that appear to be
reaching for the sky. Measuring 2 metres (7 feet) in height,
the shells are laminated in mahogany and the seat is
upholstered in leather with a solid wooden footrest below.
Halogen spotlights fitted either side of the curved tops
sparkle dramatically at night.

Gebrane's love of things musical is evident in the furniture,
which at first glance appears to be rows of marble
blocks and timber boxes. On closer inspection, the latter
resemble musical instrument cases, or even coffins,
although they are actually used as dancing platforms.
These steel-framed, mahogany boxes have an integrated
key locking device and open up to become sofas and
chairs with plush, red velvet padded seats. In contrast to
the decadent velvet and wood, the floor is finished with
durable concrete block pavement, reminding guests that
this is a space that transforms from an inside one to an
outside one.

The white block tables resemble tombstones in memory of
various musical legends, with their fixed, solid mahogany
picture frames displaying portraits of heroes such as
Charles Mingus, Miles Davis, Billie Holiday and Charlie
Parker. The aluminium vase and candlestick set into the
top, with a rose and candle replaced every night, add to
the shrine-like quality. However, after dark, these hollow
blocks come to life and become glowing light boxes.

The roof is the crowning glory – the steel structure
comprises five segments, one flap and four sliding panels,
activated by hydraulic pistons. When the sides slide back,
an expanse of sky is revealed to those below, whilst the
26 square metre (280 square foot) mirrored flap above the
bar elevates to a fixed angle, capturing a myriad outside
images – the lights of the parking carousel and those of
the speeding motorway traffic, and beyond that the
buildings in the 'Rivers' quarter of the city, mixed with an
aerial view of the club itself. To the passing motorist the
club projects the life, colour and energy from within. You
could say that B 018 really does blow the roof off.

The Bomb

Opposite:
There are two dance floors and three bars, but also smaller areas with no loudspeakers, where clubbers can talk and relax, away from the dance-floor action.

Right and far right:
Concealed lighting, together with a digital lighting system that washes the interior with changing colours, brings this subterranean labyrinth to life.

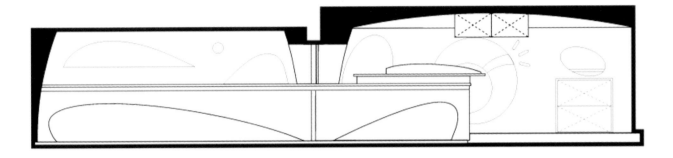

Plan:
Starting with the original shell, Lief Design chose curved shapes and forms to soften the existing harsh wall angles, creating varying levels and low ceilings.

Smouldering deep in the bowels of Bridle Gate, Nottingham, is The Bomb nightclub. Originally a network of Victorian shop cellars hollowed from sandstone, this warren of underground spaces has been a club venue since 1965. Prior to its reincarnation as The Bomb – orchestrated by Lief Design – it was a dark and dingy jazz club called The Hippo. Martin Vicker and Andy Harwood of Lief were asked to give the space a complete overhaul and create something timeless and unique. They, in turn, proposed to improve use and circulation. Major structural alterations were undertaken to open up the space. Lief stripped out the old club fittings and worked from the original shell; toilets were relocated in the lower basement; openings were widened where possible; and columns were removed and beams strengthened.

Curved lines and shapes were chosen to soften the existing haphazard wall angles, varying levels and low ceilings. The new interior was constructed like the hull of a ship and built using formers and thin marine ply-cladding, which hides the sound system and ventilation. The final layout consists of five interconnecting caves, including two dance floors and three bars. The space is accessible via stairs from the entrance at ground level and holds up to 500 clubbers.

Lief whitewashed the interior using Breplasta, a durable substance consisting of white marble, dolomide rock and latex, which is more commonly used in prisons. The Breplasta was applied with a spray gun to create a variety of textured effects. York stone was laid in the main dance area and the softer Dalsouple rubber flooring throughout the rest of the club. Smaller areas were created for those wanting to relax and chat rather than join the dance floor action. Free of speakers, they house upholstered curved benches, simple Prince Aha stools by Philippe Starck and bespoke tables-cum-light boxes made from recycled plastic.

It is the concealed lighting that brings the arches and vaulting of this funky cocoon to life. Lief devised a digital lighting system that rotates the lights, washing the interior with changing colours. Diffused light, from gelled halogen spotlights concealed behind circular forms, makes intimate areas glow red or a cool blue. The result is an intriguing igloo-like effect, which glows with strong, vibrant colours – a futuristic labyrinth for millennial clubbing.

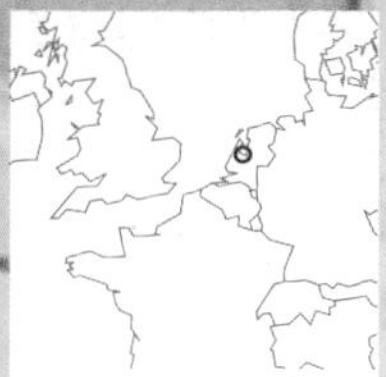

The Supperclub

Amsterdam, Netherlands
Concrete, 1999

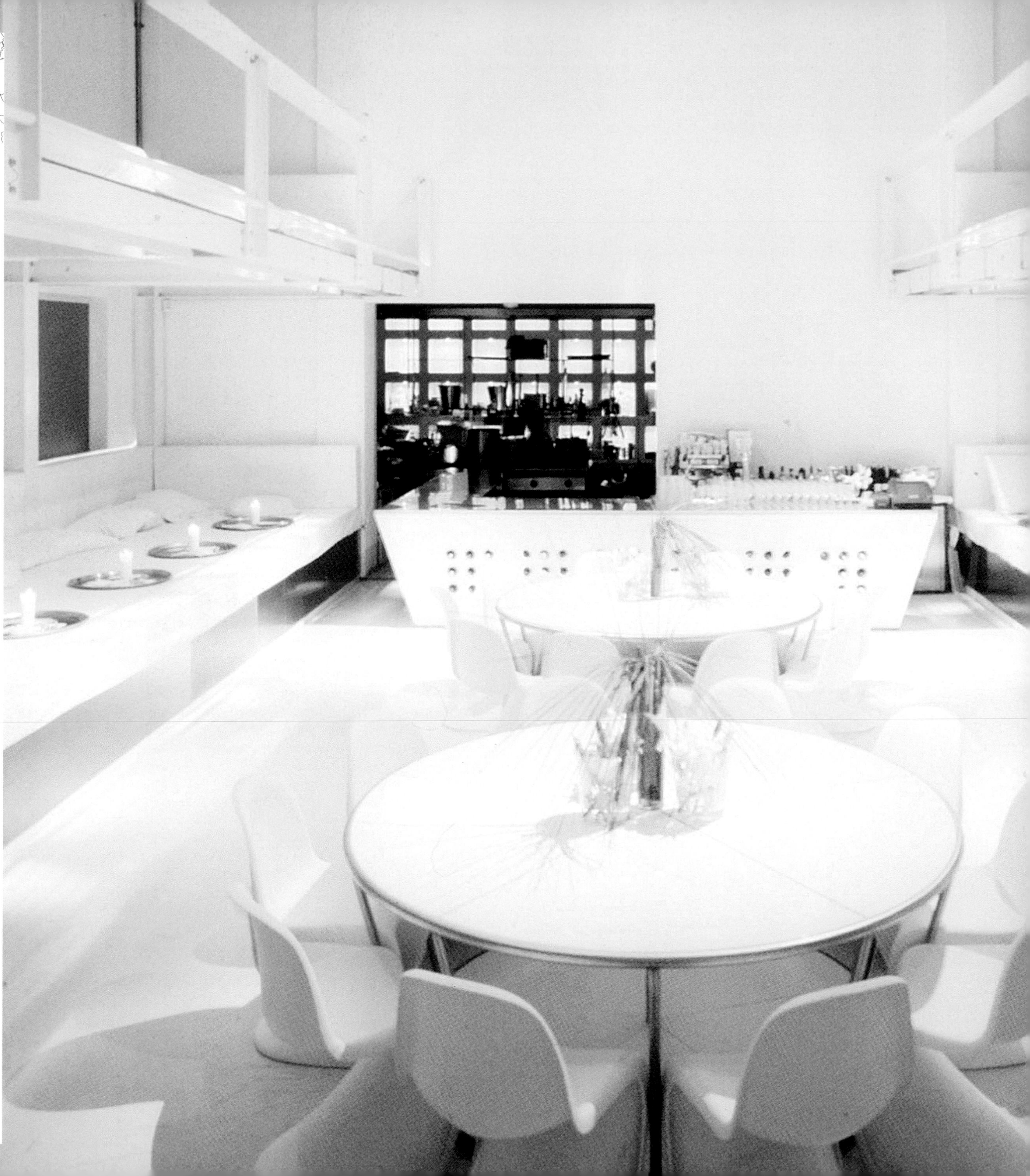

Main image left:
Shoe-free dining on two levels: guests recline on beds in an all-white environment, which is bathed in various pastel shades of light.

Right:
Downstairs, a row of three-deep booths provides intimate seating for bar-goers.

Dining at the Supperclub is a louche affair. Forget conventional tables and chairs – the majority of diners recline against large, white pillows on white mattresses, soaking up the pastel lighting as it changes colour. Two large steel structures (powder-coated in white) and positioned either side of the main room accommodate most of the diners. They must remove their shoes before climbing up onto the communal platforms, which look like two giant bunk beds. The ritual of taking off one's shoes breaks down inhibitions and adds to the chilled-out, lounge atmosphere.

Like many other exciting night-time venues, the entrance to the Supperclub is as anonymous as that of a speakeasy. The entrance consists of a single door with small brass nameplates, tucked down a cobbled alleyway in the centre of town. Guests ring a bell to gain access. Amsterdam-based design team Concrete, co-owned by Rob Wagemans and Gilian Schrofer, were responsible for the Supperclub's current incarnation. According to Wagemans, the 18th-century building was originally a tearoom, which, in the early 1990s, became a shop. For the past seven years, it has been a restaurant, attracting an arty clientele. When it was sold to a new owner a couple of years ago, Concrete were approached and commissioned to make it 'more profitable and trendy' within the overarching concept of 'lying down eating'. The building's listed status prevented Concrete from altering the internal architecture, so they formed the double-

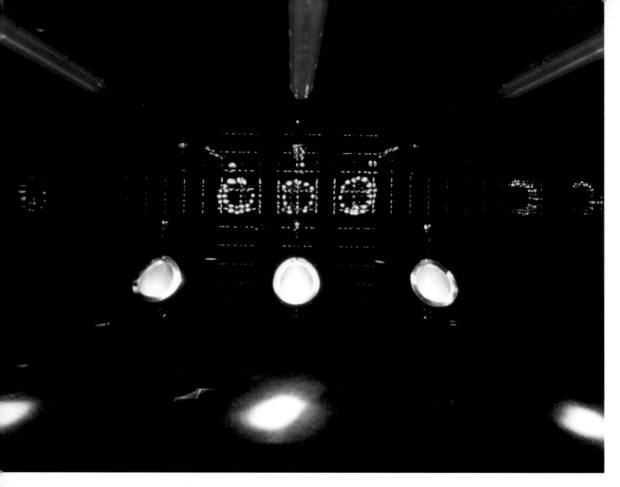

decker beds as self-supporting structures, making the upper level accessible via a stepladder, with translucent steps, fixed to the framework.

VJ and DJ booths were added and a large screen was placed above the kitchen's serving hatch. One half of the serving counter is a hot plate, allowing large numbers of plates to be prepared at once. Staff jump up onto the corner of the counter to pass dishes up to colleagues waiting to serve the top-bunk diners. Guests eat either on their laps or from silver tray-like tables, which are positioned at intervals along the mattresses. There is conventional table dining available at the centre of the room, with simple, white circular tables and white Verner Panton chairs.

In the small lobby space outside the dining room, a winding marble staircase leads down to the Red Bar, which accommodates about 60 people. Toilets are labelled 'Hetero' and 'Homo', rather than the conventional 'Ladies' and 'Gentlemen'. Wagemans explains that the restrooms are uniformly black 'because you need a lot of guts to meet people in the white room, so we made the toilets more of a meeting place.' This may explain why you find glass portholes, lit with bar bulbs, much like dressing room vanity mirrors, above the wash basins instead of mirrors. They allow guests passing through the corridor to the Red Bar a glimpse of rendez-vous candidates.

Wagemans describes the Red Bar as the 'déjà vu of the place'. There are 1960s-style red curtains, a large glowing 'BAR' sign and go-go girl-style poles, which originally were part of a bulky support wall that Concrete broke into smaller columns to maintain the atmosphere. Apparently, plenty of guests like to dance around the poles, affirming Wagemans's explanation of Concrete's design philosophy: 'We try to get more out of people than you normally do.' Beyond the bar is a white space containing four deep booths with vinyl banquettes and curtains that line the walls. Again, everything is white, providing a blank canvas for changing lighting effects.

Although the Supperclub is ostensibly a restaurant, its DJs and live music also make it a 'nightclub' experience. By the end of the night, guests can often be found dancing all over the beds. It is a piece of escapism, as Wagemans says, 'a place to forget all your sorrows'. Indeed, the ultimate come-down hits you as you pay and prepare to depart. The Supperclub inspired B.E.D. in Miami, another boudoir dining club, and further Supperclubs are planned for London and Rome, much to the delight of doyens of the night scene.

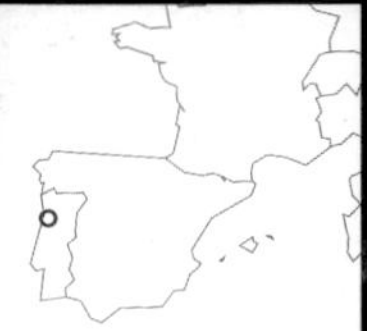

Matosinhos, Portugal
Alvarinho Siza, 1998

Next

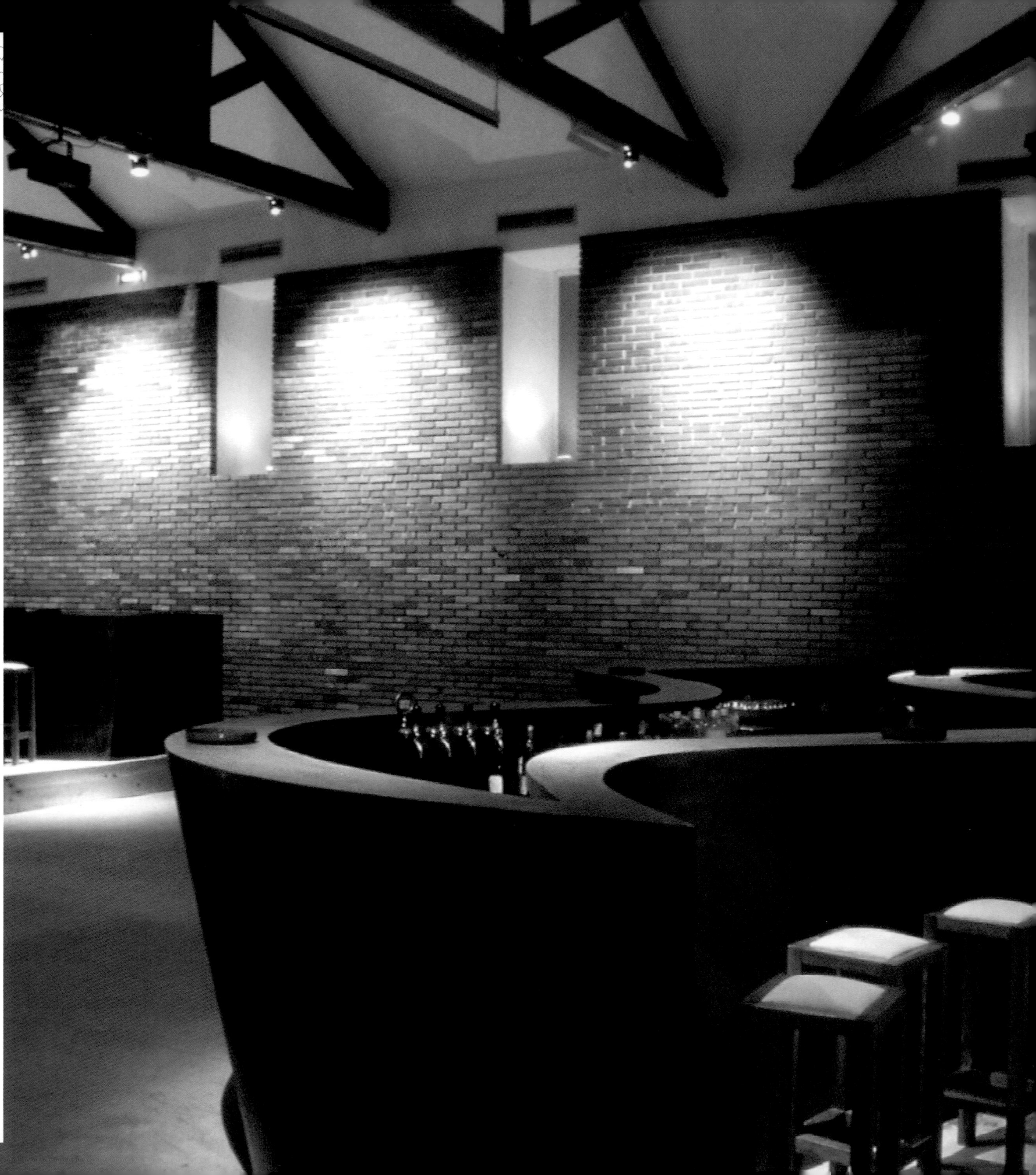

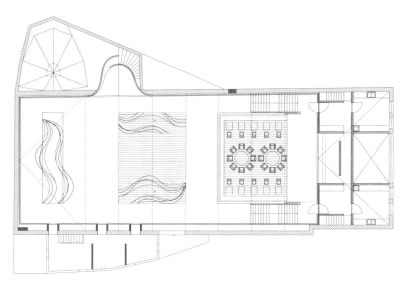

Main image left:
Curved bars, inspired by the sculptures of Richard Serra, stand out against the bare, 'less is more' exposed brick and wood of the warehouse-style club.

Plan:
Next consists of a large nave, containing three free-standing bars, and two smaller adjoining buildings.

Right:
The entrance lobby features an unusual ceiling that resembles the aperture of a camera, revealing a chink of daylight or night sky.

Ever since the late 1970s and early 1980s, new nightclubs have often been created in disused industrial spaces – empty warehouses, railway arches and lofts. This trend originated in the USA, with seminal gay and early house clubs, such as The Loft and Paradise Garage in Manhattan, New York, and the Music Box in Chicago, clubs that went on to inspire Ben Kelly in his design of Manchester's legendary Haçienda and, in turn, the creators of London's Ministry of Sound. These spaces were not about flashy, opulent decor or design, but simply about offering the very best in sound quality and music technology. They were places where the music took control, where people danced until dawn, often fuelled by various drugs.

Although the cocktail lounge has had a renaissance and there is a clearly identifiable vogue for luxuriously designed bars, the tradition of the exposed brick, raw industrial dance club continues to exist, with London clubs such as Fabric, or lounge-warehouse mutations such as Lot 61 in New York and Lux (see page 164) in Lisbon. Portugal's Next is a direct descendant of the early industrial dance clubs. The architect Alvarinho Siza's brief was to 'recreate the splendid and original spatiality of the building', which was built as a warehouse. Hence the internal walls of bare brick, chosen to conceal the ventilation pipes and cables, and to optimize the space's acoustics and act as effective soundproofing.

Next consists of a large nave with two smaller adjoining buildings – one houses the main entrance and the other the staff offices. Externally, the club has the air of a barn, with a simple doorway and plain, sandy plastered exterior. The intention was to ensure the building remained in keeping with the historic area in Matosinhos in which it stands. The budget was tight, so Siza took a 'less is more' approach, highlighting the qualities of the extant nave, choosing durable materials, such as concrete and pinewood for the floor, and metal for the bars.

The inspiration for Next came from a variety of sources, according to Siza, 'from a discothèque called Estado Novo [one of his own projects] and from the works of John Pawson, Donald Judd and Richard Serra'. The curved bars were influenced in particular by the sculptures of Serra, their soft curves emphasized by their austere surroundings. 'The traditional architecture of brick walls of the United States and the anonymous architecture of UK' also inform Siza's work, he says. This may explain the visual similarities between Next and the original, industrial clubs of 20 years ago.

London, UK
Satmoko Ball, 1998

Chinawhite

Just when Londoners were beginning to despair at the
thought of another monochrome 'modern classic', along
came an exotic wave of bars and clubs decorated in
lavish, decadent styles, arriving to save the UK capital
from minimalism fatigue. Chinawhite was one of these
new arrivals, opening in 1998 and unleashing a feast of
raw silk, rich colours and oriental artefacts across a
sprawling basement space, but only for those lucky
enough to cross the well-guarded 'red rope' threshold.
Situated close to Piccadilly Circus, an area known for its
nightlife, the low-key entrance is marked by a small
window display set into the wall, containing the Chinese
symbol of prosperity, a motif that is repeated throughout
the interior.

From the entrance, the limestone-tiled stairway leads
down to the main lobby where guests can opt to turn left
into the main room or right into the Wu Wu chill-out, or
private party, room. Interior designer Cara Satmoko of
Satmoko Ball has kept the connecting corridor natural
and, in keeping with the Asian theme, the corridor wall is
constructed from sandy-hued limestone bricks, each one
a hand-carved replica of the prosperity symbol.

The main room, which features a teak parquet floor,
offers an abundance of colour with Balinese parasols,
raw silk cushions strewn across upholstered banquettes
and Indonesian teak furniture and diaphanous drapes
adorning Bedouin-style alcoves, containing daybeds
and yet more cushions. A series of Balinese-inspired

Plan:
The sprawling basement club has
one main room with two bars, plus
two additional rooms – the Wu Wu,
with its own bar, and the VIP Mao
Room, with ensuite WC. Alll rooms
have raised seating areas.

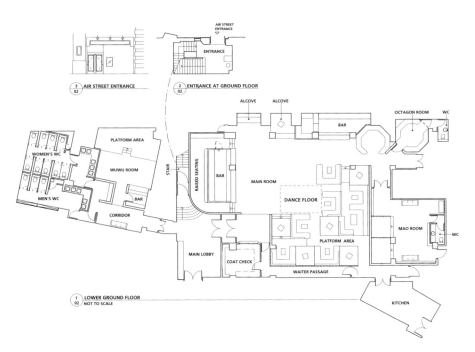

raised seating platforms accommodates small, low candle-lit tables and creates differing levels and multiple sight lines. There are two limestone bars – the main one has a raised seating area tucked behind it and features an intricate hand-carved façade.

Beyond the main room is the VIP Mao Room, which accommodates 50 guests and has its own sound system and en suite toilet. Antique Chinese furniture provides more formal seating, decor is authentic with the seating platform framed by elaborately carved screens and the walls are lacquered in shiny black. Traditional Chinese artwork is mixed with a more modern Warhol-inspired portrait of Mao Tse Tung. Opposite this room is the Octagon Snug, a cosy area that seats up to 14 people. Described by Chinawhite's owners as a 'tented jewel box', it comes complete with its own Buddha head and can be connected up to either the sound system in the Mao Room or the one in the main room.

The Wu Wu Room is located en route to the toilets and away from the main area. Simple in layout, it has a small bar and raised platform at the back, which is covered in richly patterned rugs and silken cushions making informal reclining the only option. The laid-back feel is enhanced by the tent-like material suspended from the ceiling, the lanterns and low lighting giving the space the appearance of an eastern version of a souk. Satmoko Ball have carried the Asian theming through to the washrooms, where water runs from the taps and trickles over long, trench-like basins filled with pebbles. In attempting to create 'a club unlike any other clubs' for her client, it appears that Cara Satmoko has left no stone unturned.

Opposite
Hand-carved timber doors
displaying the club's leitmotif open
into the Wu Wu Room.

Top left:
The Octagon Snug, described as a
'tented jewel box', comes complete
with its own Buddha head.

Jazz Matazz

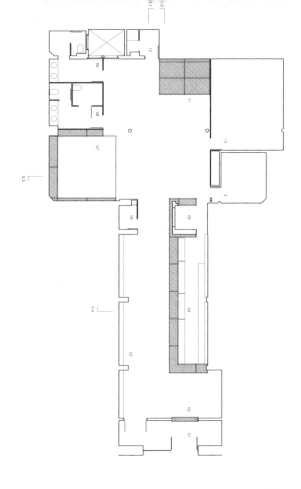

Lluis Jubert and Eugenia Santacana's renovation of this bar is a fine example of innovative thinking and a testimony to how dramatic results can be achieved in spite of a minimal budget and strict time constraints. Their brief was to 'reform the existing bar', located in a new suburb of Barcelona, whilst 'maintaining the current licence and completely changing the image of the bar'. The new bar has been reborn as Jazz Matazz, a music bar that hosts live acts and the occasional exhibition. The architectal duo inherited an uneven, awkwardly shaped, ground-floor space and so decided to create four glowing structures that would bathe the interior in warm light and provide both a theatrical setting and a backdrop against which the figures of the guests, staff and musicians would be silhouetted.

These illuminated amber-hued constructions are simple but effective, highlighting the areas of importance against the surrounding walls and ceilings, which have been coated in a dark-blue, plastic paint. Each of the four structures, described by Jubert-Santacana as 'big windows which catch the public's eye', have been constructed from colourless panes of laminated glass secured within a framework of square, stainless-steel tubes, soldered together. It is the orange, adhesive wrapping paper, attached to the back of the glass, which defines the texture, colour and light, the latter coming from adjustable, flexible lighting tubes located behind the opaque panels. From a distance, the backlit orange paper looks like a far more luxurious material, such as delicate parchment or lightly grained wood.

Guests first encounter the 'display' that supports the bar's nameplate, which is situated at the entrance, 2 metres (6½ feet) from the façade. Once inside, the most striking element by far is the 11 metre (36 foot) long bar, with only the actual counter and bottles on the uplit shelves of the back bar providing any colour. This structure also houses the DJ booth at the far end, concealed behind panelling that stretches from floor to ceiling. Towards the rear of the venue, the space opens up – tucked around to the left, opposite the bar, is the 'show room', a square enclosure that is sectioned off by a transparent screen, which functions as a kind of exhibition space. The slightly raised stage occupies a prime corner position, in line with the bar and surrounded by plenty of space for dancing.

Man Ray

Main image left:
The cavernous interior is enriched by Asian-influenced details, from the colourful mandala ceiling panels to the Indian musician figureheads and the serene busts that grace the two large ottomans.

Above:
The bar is on the mezzanine level. The multicoloured glasswork of the bar top and back bar panels complement the rich colours elsewhere.

Portuguese-born, Parisian-based architect and designer Miguel Cancio Martins has created a succession of *bonnes boîtes* from the Med to LA, all proving extremely popular with celebrity jet-setters and the world's party people. Earlier Parisian projects include Barfly and the much-touted Buddha Bar, which spawned the popular series of CDs. Man Ray, located near to the Champs Elysées, has probably received more column inches for its famous investors – Simply Red lead singer Mick Hucknall and film actors Johnny Depp and Sean Penn – than for its design. It seems apt that the subterranean site was formerly a cinema. Martins was asked to create a 'bar-restaurant with an Asian touch' that could also accommodate large parties. Apart from this, he was given carte blanche for the design.

Despite occupying a basement, Man Ray is a grand, cavernous venue, with the bar area situated on a mezzanine level and a balcony that wraps around the outside of the room, allowing drinkers the opportunity to gaze upon the diners seated below. Twin staircases curve down from the bar to the restaurant below and, on the opposite side of the dining room, a pool clad in Moroccan, turquoise-blue ceramic tiles provides a cool, calming visual respite from the pastel orange walls and rich, gold-leaf pillars that surround the dining area. Two huge models of Indian musicians protrude, like figureheads, from the wall at either side of the pool, which can be covered to form a

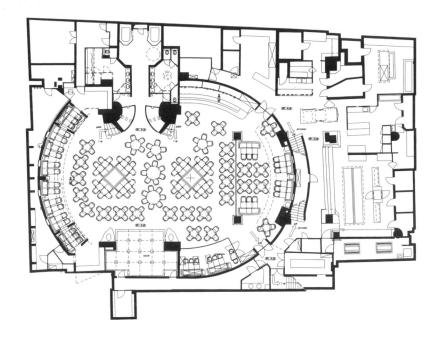

stage for live music events. There is also a DJ booth on the balcony and, on certain nights of the week, tables around the pool are removed to provide an area for dancing.

Four custom-designed, fabric chandeliers, dripping with trimmings, draw the eye upwards to the main feature, the stunning stained-glass, backlit ceiling panels, which display a circular mandala symbol. Echoes of this central motif can be seen elsewhere in Man Ray, such as in the circular design of the balcony and staircase balustrade and in the multicoloured glass panels of the back bar and bar counter tops. Furniture is bespoke and modelled on luxury Asian hotel pieces – low lounge chairs and sofas in the bar are upholstered in jade and yellow fabrics decorated in oriental writing. In the restaurant, the symmetrical seating layout is dominated by two extremely large ottomans, each with padded backs and crowned with a trio of serene-looking Asian figureheads. This theatrical bar-restaurant is designed for people who want to see and be seen. From the upper balcony to descending the grand staircase, everything about it encourages voyeurism.

Rome, Italy
Claudio Lazzarini and Carl Pickering, 2000

Bar Nil

Opposite:
The bar occupies an oval space,
encircled by sheer white curtains.
The mirrored bar façade reflects
and accentuates the various
lighting effects.

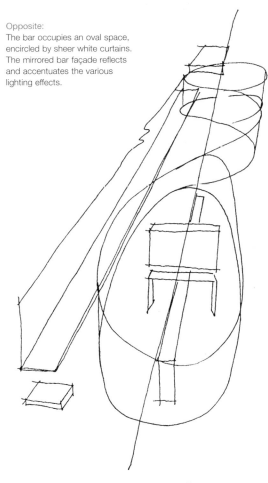

Sketch:
This graphic representation of the
venue shows the fluidity of
space, created by a series of
electronically operated curtains.

Above left and right:
Video images of different colours
and patterns, projected onto the
white drapes, create changes in
mood and atmosphere.

The boundaries between nightclub, café, restaurant and bar have become blurred. It is no longer enough to provide an environment geared towards only one activity; the cosmopolitan, modern consumer expects choice. In response to this, operators are keen to create venues where a night's entertainment can include dining, drinking and dancing in one seamless experience. It maximizes their profits and keeps the party going longer. The design of Bar Nil, in Rome, exemplifies this 'multiple-purpose' approach.

Architects Claudio Lazzarini and Carl Pickering were asked to create 'a bar/restaurant that worked well from aperitif time to dancing in the early hours…with an international atmosphere'. Their design fulfils this brief using flexible systems that include electrical curtains, lighting and video projections. These systems allow different perspectives to be created and help to establish separate areas within the space, without losing the overall atmosphere. The name 'Nil' was chosen to express the concept of the venue as a 'blank page on which to write, spatially and geographically', say Lazzarini and Pickering. They have laid out a clean, white slate on which to project different atmospheres and moods through colours, patterns and images.

The interior is pure and simple with plenty of white surfaces and natural stone, so as not to detract from its function as a backdrop. Flooring is light in tone – marble dust-and-resin tiles – and furniture includes white vinyl banquettes, unimposing stainless steel Bertoia chairs, blocks of Roman travertine and a pine bench. The elongated, rectilinear public space can be divided into three consecutive areas that flow into each other. As the evening progresses, these are gradually opened up and Bar Nil becomes one. The first space is the bar, formed by two narrow bar counters, which overlap in the shape of the cross. A mirrored bar façade reflects and accentuates all lighting changes and projections. The bottle display in the back bar occupies minimal space – just a narrow shelf in white board, which does not interrupt the blank canvas quality of the interior. A projection screen hangs above the bar and diaphanous white curtains can be activated electronically to form an oval enclosure around this drinking area.

The bleached-pine bench lining the left-hand wall functions as a raised walkway connecting the various areas – a bench for diners in the restaurant and, later on in the evening, a platform for dancing. In the restaurant, banquettes line the opposite wall, curving around and demarcating the bar from the dining area. White drapes line both walls, on which video projections create

atmospheric changes – from simple pink or blue hues to acidic optical or polka-dot patterns and moving images of water or fire. Computer-controlled, halogen ceiling lighting adds to these effects; it can make the space appear to pulsate or can be used to highlight particular areas.

At the far end of the space there is a DJ booth and stage. Here again, diaphanous drapes can be activated to create a separate area for private dining. There is no 'official' dance floor – guests dance in any available space, including on the bench and travertine blocks, until Bar Nil closes in the early hours of the morning.

Astro

The outdoors indoors – Michael Young describes the main bar as a 'sort of swimming pool crossed with picnic area concept'.

Above:
The bar is moulded from glacier-white corian, a man-made stone composite similar to marble.

Right:
View of the bar from the sunken Smarty Pool, which was inspired by the geothermal areas of Iceland.

Reykjavik, Iceland – place of quirky pop stars, long nights and hot springs – is the setting and inspiration for the DJ bar Astro. The funky, technicolour interior was created after restructuring one of Reykjavik's oldest buildings (90 years old). British-born designer Michael Young began by observing Icelandic craftsmanship: 'They are extremely good…especially at concrete and steelwork, which is used in swimming pools and geothermal areas in Iceland.' Young decided to bring 'the outdoors indoors' and to utilize these local craft skills in the creation of Astro. Hence the final layout of the main bar with its low lounge chairs and picnic bench tables positioned around the sunken Smarty Pool. Young describes this as 'a sort of swimming pool crossed with a picnic area concept'.

Young created most of the furniture and lighting products and is responsible for the curved shapes, futuristic forms, synthetic materials and vibrant colours that make Astro a surreal environment. There are two floors, a bar and dance floor downstairs, and a private room and bar-dancefloor above. DJs play on both floors. The bars are moulded from glacier-white corian, a man-made stone composite, similar to marble, and the floor surface throughout is a resin-based compound. In the main bar, the Red Button, Smarty cushions appear like a fleet of mini-flying saucers lying in a crater. Officially known as MY16, the cushions were created by Young from self-skinning foam and have been produced by Italian manufacturer Cappellini since

1998. The stools, lounge chairs and Young's trademark
magazine sofa, MY03, are all constructed with chrome
steel frames and upholstered in white leather and have
been manufactured by Cappellini and Sawaya & Moroni.

Aside from the weird and wonderful forms and textures,
it is the lighting that truly sends Astro into hyperspace.
Lighting designer Jeremy Lord has devised a colour-
changing lighting system behind the bar counter, its
effect maximized by Young's inclusion of intermittent white
walls among the aqua green, which reflect the changing
spectrum of hues. Then there are Young's space-age
Sticklights – manufactured by Eurolounge in rotation
moulded plastic – positioned around the periphery of
the room, which emit a glow that varies in colour
depending on the filters fitted inside.

Upstairs, Astro takes on even stranger colours. The
ambient dance floor exudes a range of hues from a
Jeremy Lord Colourwall and the more relaxed, private
members' room features walls that actually change colour.
The aptly titled Red Room has heat-sensitive walls, which
contain light insets and thermo-formed polycarbonate
plastic – they start out a pale pink and intensify to a deep
red the busier the room becomes. In a country with long,
cold winters Young's artificial outdoors-indoors, full of
light and colour, must go down a storm.

Embassy

James Bond would feel very much at home in the retro-chic surroundings of Embassy. This multi-purpose venue, in the Sydney suburb of Double Bay, exudes a 1960s glamour, with its earthy colours and white, curved forms. Architects McconnellRayner were asked to design a 'lounge atmosphere with a hint of fantasy Eastern Bloc' in what was formerly a restaurant and function space. Their completed interior features areas devoted to dining, drinking, dancing and lounging for up to 650 people.

Like many modern establishments, Embassy was conceived with flexibility in mind – the owners asked that the project be adaptable, so it could be used as 'a club/lounge/dance venue, as well as a place for lunch and fashion parades'. McconnellRayner have managed to include all these desired aspects by creating different sections within the venue. The DJ booth, dance floor and large 'island' bar dominate the central area, with an entire corner of the space devoted to the bar and surrounding seating. The dance floor, positioned off-centre, is defined by an oval of parquetry flooring, which contrasts with the charcoal carpet. Nightclub-style lighting is located in a shallow 'ceiling dome' directly above the dance floor.

A second counter bar overlooks the dance floor, which serves to separate the restaurant and supper club from the nightclub and lounge area. The long dining area lines the wall. In the opposite corner is the Cigar Lounge – this intimate room, with its own bar, can be completely closed off, or the doors can be slid back to connect it with the

Main image left:
The most eye-catching features are the booths, framed by 1960s-inspired, white screens, and the luminous, square bar, made from a translucent material, backlit by warm, white neon.

Above:
Deep-red, padded walls curve up over guests' heads in the bar's intimate booths. Greater privacy is achieved by drawing the silver, mesh-metal curtains across the entrance aperture.

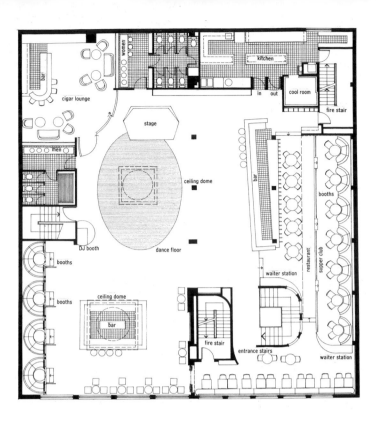

main space. McconnellRayner have achieved a luxurious lounge feel by carpeting the entire space (apart from the dance floor), and introducing soft lines and finishes wherever possible, such as the curved, padded vinyl wall in the supper club. Further refinement is produced by the calm, muted colours and the comfortable booth seating.

The white, luminous main bar and circular-framed booths are by far the most impressive, eye-catching feature of Embassy. All the bar material has been constructed from Marblo – a translucent, solid material – which is backlit by warm, white neon, so the counter and corners of the large central bar glow brightly. The counter façade is clad in Broadline glass, with an interlayer of iridescent paint, backed with mirror, to create a silvery appearance. Glittering directly above the bar, suspended from a square coffer, is a 1960s chandelier. Part of the original venue's decor, it adds to the sense of retro-glam.

The four, slightly raised, booths overlooking the bar are deeply appealing places to be. They are framed by large, circular apertures that are carved out of the white, polystyrene screen, which echo the circular windows of the nearby wall. The screen is carved into shape and then coated with polyester resin to ensure durability. Inside, semi-circular banquettes curve around a single table and deep-red upholstered walls wrap up behind guests'

heads. Atmospheric uplighting emphasizes the cocoon-like form of these intimate spaces. Privacy is possible through the drawing of silver, mesh metal curtains – an ideal spot for a martini-sipping 007 and his girls, perhaps?

Lux

Lisbon, Portugal
Manuel Reis, Fernando Fernandes
and José Miranda, 1998

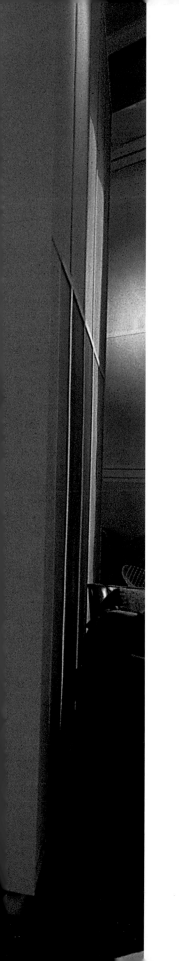

Main image left:
The huge wall panels can be
slid into various positions,
allowing the interior to mutate
without losing its distinctive
open-plan feel.

Above left and right:
This loft-warehouse club,
overlooking Lisbon's River
Tagus, occupies one of the first
concrete structures ever built
in the city's docks.

Lux follows a tradition of clubs that are located off the
beaten track in deserted industrial wastelands or in
spaces converted from disused railway viaducts or power
stations – dormant warehouses reborn for the pursuit of
pleasure rather than labour and toil. Indeed, this late-night
lounge bar and club could be in any city in the world –
London, New York, Chicago – were it not for the balcony
views of Lisbon's River Tagus. Although Lux opened in
September 1998, this loft-warehouse was one of the
first concrete structures ever built on the docks and had
been standing strong since 1910.

It was when the Port of Lisbon started planning to
rehabilitate urban areas that Manuel Reis, Fernando
Fernandes and José Miranda came up with the Lux
concept. Their aim was to resuscitate an area that had
so far been totally neglected in terms of leisure and
commercial interests. Reis already had considerable
experience in both the nightclub and design fields. He
is the highly revered founder of one of Lisbon's most
celebrated clubs – Fragil – which initiated the growth of
the Barrio Alto as the capital's hip, nightlife quarter. He
is also the owner of Loja da Atalaia in Lisbon, a stylish
shop selling retro furniture and objets.

Lux is not rigidly designed. It is like many other
contemporary nocturnal spaces – incredibly fluid and
flexible. The ground floor is devoted entirely to dancing.
It is the upstairs lounge bar, which also has a DJ, that
appeals most, with its ever-changing, candy-coloured

retro 1960s and 1970s furniture, on show and on sale
from Loja da Atalaia. Speakers are built into the huge
mobile wall panels, which can be slid into different
positions, allowing the interior to mutate without losing the
distinctive open-plan feel. These white screens reflect the
changing light, colours and patterns, and are also ideal
backdrops for video artists' work and other performers.

The simplistic, but adaptable environment generates
a laid-back, lounge atmosphere; guests can put their
chairs wherever they choose, nothing is fixed. At dawn,
the crowd gravitates towards the sliding doors and out
onto the balcony, where the cranes and mechanical
debris of the docks are silhouetted against the sun
rising over the Tagus.

Zeppelin

Moscow, Russia
Boris Ktoutik, 2000

Opposite:
A small airship – the club's emblem – appears to float at the top of the stained claret oak stairs, which provide access to Zeppelin's various levels.

Right:
Aerodynamic Hindenberg arcs are repeated throughout the space. Even the double-decker DJ cabin hovers like a shiny dirigible, surrounded by an arc of starry spotlights.

It is perhaps apt that this private Moscow club, no doubt frequented by the capital's more affluent citizens, occupies a building that was originally a house created by an 'unknown nobleman' in the 19th century. Following the October Revolution of 1917, the building was utilized for other purposes and prior to the creation of the Zeppelin was an office building. The recent transformation involved maximizing the space through extensive development of both the ground and attic floors in order to achieve a total of 1,000 square metres (10,760 square feet) spread over four levels.

The owners were keen to recreate 'the atmosphere of the legendary Hindenberg airship' and, indeed, new arrivals ascending the luminous stairway are immediately attracted to the club's emblem. Stunningly back-lit and outlined by a yellow halo, the mini-airship appears to float at the top of the stairs. In addition, the ceiling above the stairs represents the belly of a dirigible, complete with motor and rotating propeller.

Four steps up on the right is the entrance to the 'discothèque', where the majority of the space is devoted to the dance floor. However, it also boasts two bars and a lounge area. Newcomers are greeted with an aerial view, before descending a few steps that wind down around a curved, lilac wall, which leads them into the club. This wall, punctuated by a series of glass brick windows, also forms the back wall of the bar on the other side.

Aerodynamic Hindenberg arcs are repeated throughout. The entire lounge area forms an arc against the dance floor and is enclosed by a steel structure that functions as a drinking counter. Guests seated on the metal stools, covered in blue vinyl, can choose to gaze at the sofa occupants or those boogying away beneath the glitterball. Diagonally opposite, the double-decker DJ cabin hovers like some shiny silver mothership secured by steel wires and surrounded by an arc of stars. The top booth allows the DJ to play to the crowd from up on high and is accessible by a small flight of steps.

Vibrant chunks of orange, the deep blues, pinks and reds of the upholstery, and columns clad in crimson plastic enliven the cold steel elements and neutral tones of the varnished laminate floor, styled to imitate floorboards. There is a second bar at the far end of the room where guests can also sit, relax and survey the scene. Zeppelin is not simply a disco, but a veritable entertainment complex. There is also a cinema and cigar lounge on the floor above and a dining restaurant on the third floor, plus a beauty salon and sauna in the former attic. All are accessible from the main stairway.

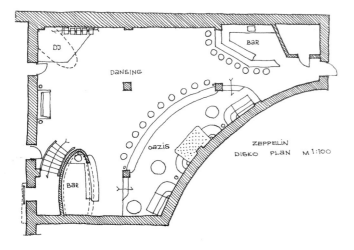

Plan:
Most of the space is devoted to the dance floor, although there is an arc-shaped lounge area, plus two bars.

Main image right:
The lounge area is enclosed by a steel structure that functions as a drinking counter, allowing guests ringside views of those dancing away beneath the glitterball.

São Paulo, Brazil
Isay Weinfeld, 2000

Disco

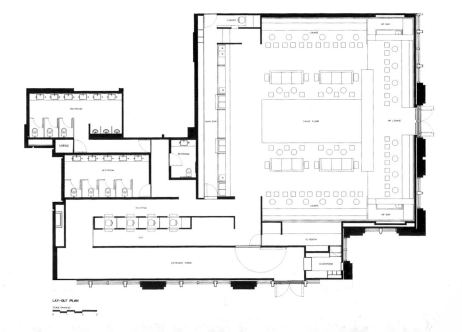

Opposite:
The word 'Disco' shines forth at the end of the mosaic-clad entrance corridor, which is lit with tiny, stellar fibre-optics. Like fiery flames in outer space, they entice clubbers into this other-wordly realm.

Above:
Neon-lit acrylic sinks glow dramatically in the darkness of the club's toilets.

If nightclubs are about both darkness and light – nocturnal spaces where individuals can get lost in the crowd and abandon themselves to the sensory pleasures of light and music – then Disco is iconic. It is located on São Paulo's vibrant Faria Lima Avenue, a street known especially for its thriving nightlife. The interior appears initially to be almost non-existent, visitors having to trip through pitch darkness, with only a few glimpses of light to guide them. Architect Isay Weinfeld was asked to create a nightclub that was 'elegant and daring', characteristics that are certainly in evidence, from the entrance to the toilets.

The long entrance tunnel is lined in tiny, multicoloured mosaic tiles, lit by randomly placed fibre-optics, which sparkle and glitter like stars in a night sky. At the end of the passageway, an orange neon sign saying 'Disco' burns brightly, reflecting against the mosaic tunnel. Disco consists of one large room, with a long, black Formica bar stretching along one side. In the centre is a rectilinear dance floor, made of black wood, with lounge seating on either side. On the opposite side of the room is a long bench, which separates the VIP area from the main space, a slightly raised area with two small bars, one at each end. Everything is uniformly black – the synthetic leather sofas, the three bars, the carpet and the walls – ensuring that any brightly coloured elements stand out.

The main focus of the room is a wall by the design duo the Campana brothers, created from hundreds of colourful plastic strings, up- and downlit and redolent of a Jackson Pollock painting. Other sources of vibrancy include the programmed lighting that changes colour, the neon acrylic bar shelves and the candy-coloured lounge stools. In the bathroom, acrylic sinks stand out against a sea of black.

Above:
The interior is almost uniformly black, apart from neon-lit acrylic details and the Jackson Pollock-like wall behind the main bar, created by designers the Campana brothers from hundreds of pieces of coloured plastic string.

Plan:
Disco consists of a square room with a central dance floor, flanked by lounge seating and with a bench at the far end, which separates the VIP area from the main space.

LAY-OUT PLAN

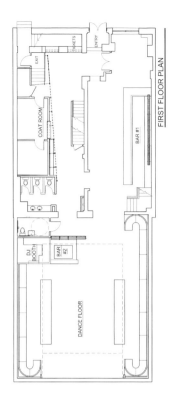

FIRST FLOOR PLAN

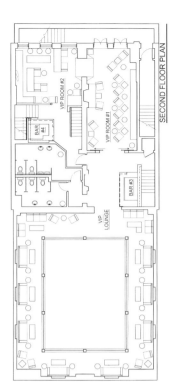

SECOND FLOOR PLAN

Manhattan-born architect and designer Jeffrey Beers is creator and co-owner of Float, a nightclub-cum-late-night lounge bar in the city's midtown theatre district. Like many club owners, Beers was inspired by the legendary Studio 54. As he told *Contract* magazine (June 2000), 'It was the energy of Studio 54 that was on my mind in creating Float, the energy, the spirit, the intensity. The idea that the evening builds.'

The 560 square metre (6,000 square foot) venue is organized over three levels. The ground floor houses two bars and main dance floor, overlooked by the VIP balcony lounge above, which also has two bars and two separate VIP rooms. Ultra-exclusive guests are given access, via a balcony enclosed in glass that wraps around the front exterior of the building and up a staircase, to the third floor, where there is another lounge bar and three more individual VIP rooms. Float displays Jeffrey Beers' talent for employing dramatic lighting and diverse materials to create contrasting areas – for example, the dance floor is dominated by cool, blue tones, but the lounge areas are wrapped up in richer gold, orange and ruby-red hues.

Beers designed the dance floor with flexibility in mind – the open space is flanked by two long banquettes and there are glowing resin plinths that function as benches earlier in the evening, but transform into dancing platforms later as the crowd trip the light fantastic. An understated Asian theme can be identified in the red disco lights suspended over the floor, which look somewhat like

Main image left:
The dance floor, overlooked by the mezzanine lounge, exhibits Asian-influenced detailing, such as the red disco lights and the backlit plexiglas wall, reminiscent of Japanese lanterns and screens.

Plan:
The venue is structured hierarchically, with the VIP balcony lounge bars on the second floor. Truly high-octane guests gain access to the ultra-exclusive lounge on the top floor via stairs and a glass-enclosed balcony that wraps around the outside of the building.

Japanese lanterns, and in the simple, grid-like squares of the balcony balustrade above and the backlit plexiglas wall panels that enclose the dance floor.

Float's upper levels contain sumptuous lounges, tailored to seduce the Big Apple's nocturnal elite. Lighting is subdued – rooms are lit moodily by candlelight, with backlit ceilings and occasional downlighting. Clean lines are plentiful, from the cube pouffes and gold leaf-coated tables to the low lounge chairs, ottomans and suede banquettes. Silk and velvet cushions in olive green, mustard yellow and burgundy add splashes of colour. During the course of the night, as the ground floor fills up, the chosen few ascend to the upper echelons, to observe the dancing bodies below.

Above:
The luminous blue plinths, either side of the dance floor, function as benches early in the evening, but later, as the crowd trips the light fantastic, they become dancing platforms.

Main image right:
In contrast to the spectacular, blue-lit main space, the VIP lounges are calmer havens of gold, mustard yellow and burgundy.

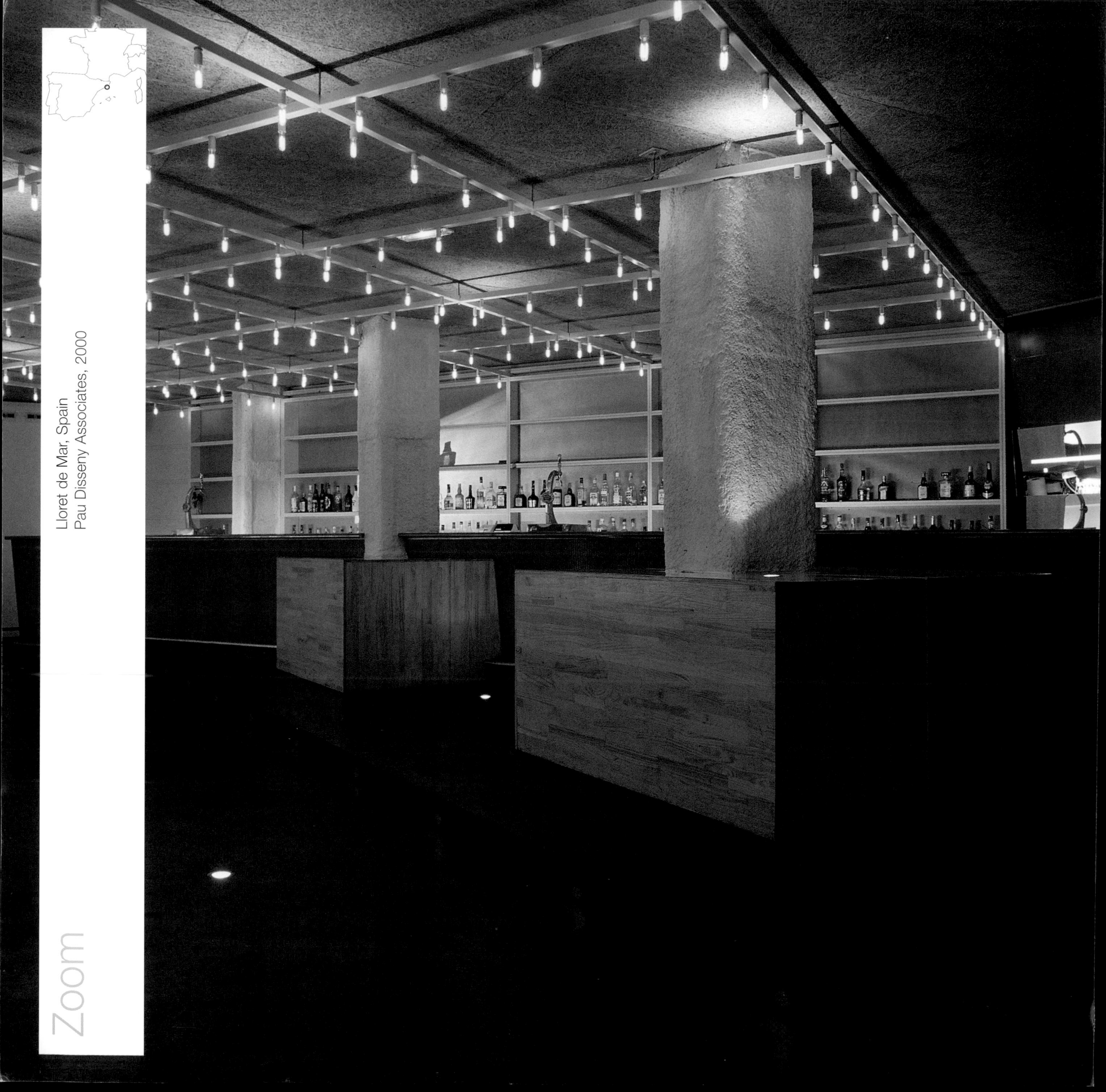

Zoom

Lloret de Mar, Spain
Pau Disseny Associates, 2000

Opposite:
The existing concrete support
columns are incorporated into
the design of the venue by
constructing slatted Galician
pinewood boxes around their
bases, thus providing additional
surfaces for drinks.

Sketch:
Pau Disseny gave the interior a
new orientation, placing the bar
at a diagonal, thus concealing
the service areas behind the
translucent parchment of the
back bar.

Right:
Soundproofing requirements
necessitated a double entrance,
so an entrance and exit lobby-
cube was created, complete with
vertical and horizontal window
slots to provide sneak previews
before entering.

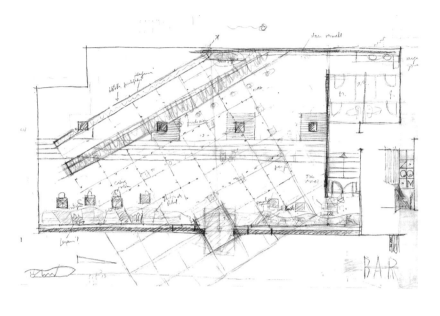

Zoom was born out of the restructuring of the Aurora Hotel in Lloret de Mar, Catalonia, Spain. The renovation of the building left an empty basement space – formerly the hotel kitchen – dominated by four square concrete columns with bulky, 1 metre (3 foot) high bases. The main entrance was through a 3 metre (10 foot) wide sliver of a gap between two other buildings next to the hotel. Interior designers Xavier Pau i Corominas and Jordi Pau i Corominas of Pau Disseny Associates were asked to transform this awkward space into a music bar.

Their design featured major changes to the exterior of the space in order to provide access from street level, which is almost 3 metres (10 feet) above the entrance. A staircase was created and a lift was installed at the rear for disabled guests. A false façade, constructed from square glass panels lined with parchment, bridges the gap between the two buildings and incorporates the neon 'ZOOM' sign. The genuine façade is lined with wooden panels and follows the incline of the stairway, exaggerating the downward perspective from the street. Two sloping canopies, one at street level and the other over the doorway, plus the tips of three cypress trees, indicate the presence of the venue. The trees are also a welcome sign in Spanish culture.

In order to achieve the maximum capacity, Pau Disseny took a somewhat oblique approach and gave the interior space a new orientation. The bar counter is placed at a diagonal and the reticular back bar shelving, with its translucent parchment backing ideal for overhead projections, separates the public space from the service areas. A square grid of 475 low-intensity bulbs suspended from the ceiling follows the proportions of the shelving, the hundreds of lights enlivening the underground space.

Soundproofing requirements necessitated a double entrance, so a huge timber box forming an almost invasive entrance and exit lobby-cube was created. Set at an angle parallel with the bar counter, horizontal and vertical window slots have been inserted. Suggestive of abstract facial features, they entice visitors into taking sneak previews before entering.

The illuminated wall either side of the entrance is composed of translucent parchment, protected by glass panels and backlit. This backlighting outlines the curves of the vinyl banquette, which features a colourful abstract representation of the Lloret beaches. All the other furniture, including chrome-plated stools, stainless-steel tables and wickerwork armchairs are lightweight and movable, allowing the space to be turned over to dancing.

Café L'Atlantique

Milan, Italy

Fabio Novembre, 1995

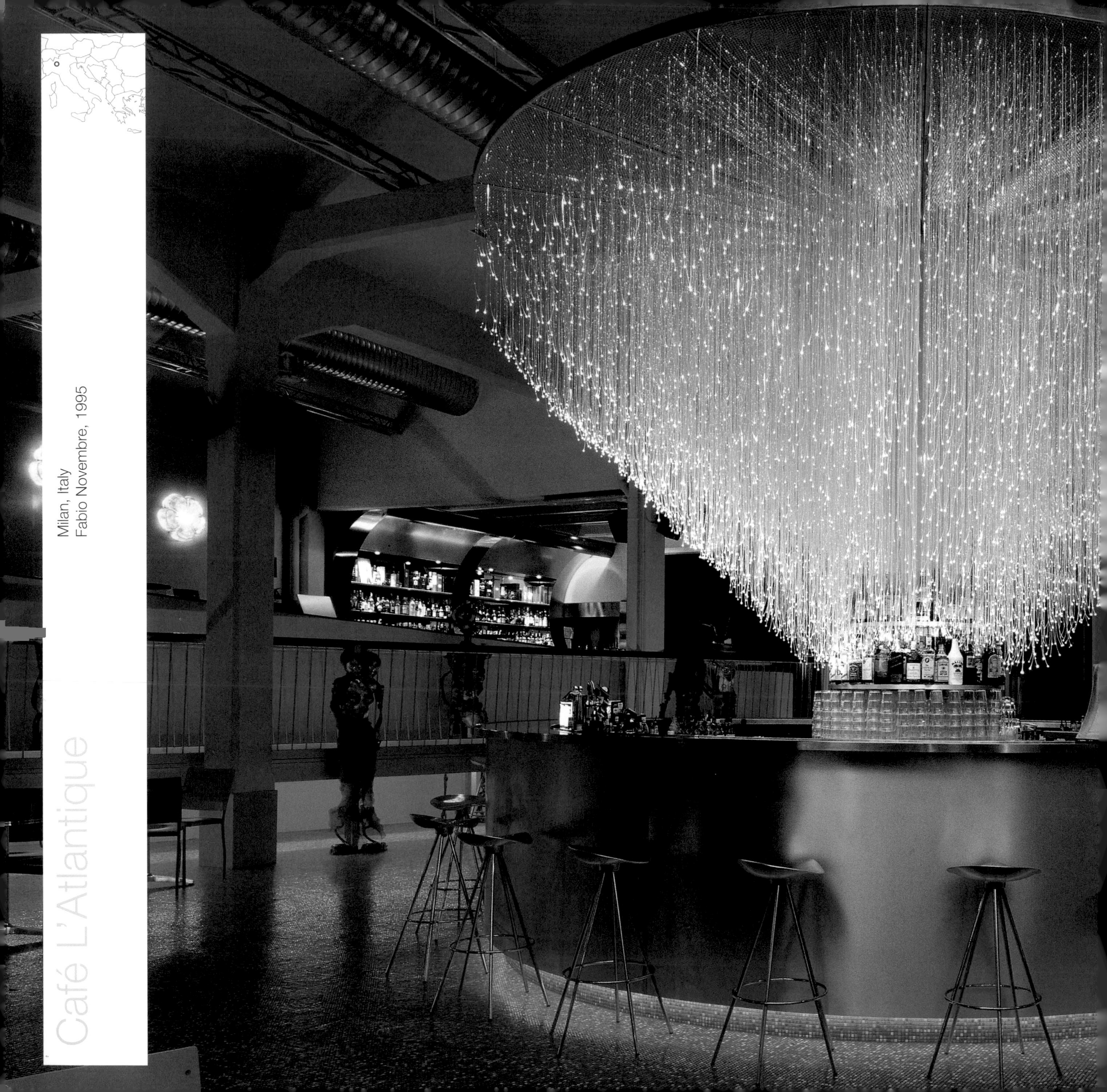

A heavenly shower of fibre-optic light tentacles forms a shimmering chandelier above the bar, making it the venue's star attraction.

Café L'Atlantique is a nightclub in a traditional sense of the word. It offers dining, drinking and dancing – all under the roof of a former industrial shed in Milan. Fabio Novembre's design is far from traditional, though. The blue mosaic floor of his bar-restaurant-discothèque has been described as a figure for the sea, with the bar itself as an atoll supporting the city's shipwrecked souls. Indeed, the island bar is the star attraction – surrounded by a pool of blue light, it appears to float in the centre of the space, with a sparkling, heavenly shower of fibre-optic light tentacles forming a shimmering chandelier above. Amongst the deep-blue tones, it is like a starry beacon offering hope to the lovelorn of the night.

Novembre's design obliterates any sense of the original rectilinearity of the space. There are several different areas surrounding the central bar, offering a variety of atmospheres and viewpoints, testimony perhaps to Novembre's training in film and his love of the medium. To the right of the entrance is the plush VIP Lounge – a baroque symphony of blue velvet with floor-to-ceiling drapes, regal gilt-framed chairs and couches. It is seductively low-lit, with ornate chandeliers that contain red bulbs, which glow like embers amidst the midnight blue.

A raised walkway stretches virtually the whole length of the main room. It is lined by android sentinels, constructed from scrap metal by the Mutoid Waste Company. They are an apocalyptic presence.

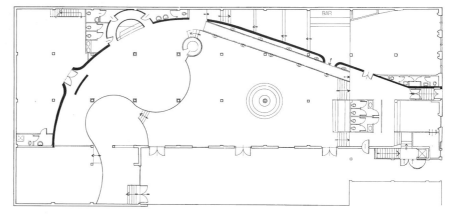

Hamel describes them as a symbol of 'this age of split identities'. It is perhaps worth noting also that Novembre's favourite film is *Blade Runner*.

The walkway forms a barrier, dividing the main bar from the mezzanine seating area, which features daisy-shaped vinyl chairs, a mosaic floor with daisy motif and matching plastic wall lamps. One theory is that this floral fantasy represents the petal-pulling riddle 'She loves me, she loves me not' – a cupid, armed with a laser rifle and perched on high, adds to this theme. The restaurant at the far end is a sea of pink and crimson, lit by yellow illuminated panelling, which surrounds the support columns. A silver vinyl version of Leonardo da Vinci's *Last Supper* decorates the wall in the intimate, private dining room. There is also an outdoor courtyard, accessible from the main bar via one of three doorways. Etched into the steel doorframes are Chinese ideograms that read 'Love grows on sex.' Is this Novembre's motto for all those at sea in Café L'Atlantique?

Above left:
The plush VIP lounge is a baroque den of blue velvet, with floor-to-ceiling drapes and regal gilt-framed sofas.

Above right and opposite:
The illuminated walkway, lined by scrap-metal androids, provides an elevated viewing point from which to look at the bar and dance floor below. It also separates the main bar from the daisy-themed seating area, which plays on the petal-pulling riddle, 'She loves me, she loves me not.'

Plan:
The creation of various different areas and levels displaces any sense of the original rectilinearity of the former industrial shed.

Opposite:
The space – almost completely white and lit by Tom Dixon's Jacklights, sliced in half to form ceiling lights – is dazzling.

Right and far right:
White sofa booths line the walls, creating a soft, cocooned interior. The DJ booth is tucked away in a corner, surrounded by an illuminated dance floor.

Plan
There are two bars – the main island Take-Off Bar and the smaller Bubble Bar. One-way windows line the internal walls, allowing guests to peruse the crowd on the X-Ray dance floor below.

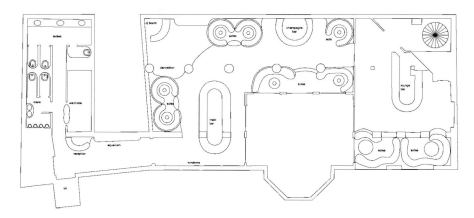

NASA is a futuristic white wonderland of a club, located in the centre of Copenhagen in an early 18th-century building, which has been converted into a commercial mews. It is situated on the first floor with two further venues, belonging to the same owners, The Fever and Slide (formerly X-Ray and Le Kitch), located below on the mezzanine level and ground floor respectively.

Turbo2000's design brief was to create 'Europe's most stylish nightclub', a place where the cosmopolitan international community of professionals working in the fashion, arts, media and entertainment industries could hang out and party. Part-owner Johannes Torpe was responsible for the sound, graphics and lighting, but everything else, from the toilet doors to the dance floor is bespoke, created by Turbo2000.

Guests are 'beamed up' to the first floor in an external glass elevator, where access to the exclusive NASA is gained by producing a white bar-coded membership card or by flashing an invitation in the form of a pocket torch at the doorman. They then enter a 1960s-style synthetic environment of pure white forms. In keeping with the bleached backdrop, albescent Japanese Koi fish inhabit the 3-metre long aquarium that lines the entrance corridor, and staff are, of course, dressed in white. It is the patrons that add colour, as their clothes and bodies are reflected in the shiny surfaces of epoxy resin, matt latex, fibreglass, plastic and vinyl.

The U-shaped space features the main Take-Off Bar, which serves beers, and the smaller Bubble Bar serving champagne and cigars, plus a raised, illuminated dance floor and corner DJ booth. Virtually every wall is lined with banquette booths, creating a soft, cocoon-like atmosphere. One-way windows line the walls, allowing members to peruse the crowd on the X-Ray dance floor below. NASA literally glows – what is not white is illuminated by numerous light sources, from the Tom Dixon Jacklights on the ceiling, looking like UFOs in flight, to the ambient lighting panels built into the walls, bar fronts, sofa booths and toilet mirrors. The overall effect is that of a spacecraft interior. There are plans to expand the concept and in the future we might see NASAs landing elsewhere around the world.

Caribou Hangar Bar

Main image left:
The propeller of the disassembled Caribou plane juts out at the end of the main bar, like a huge industrial fan.

Plan:
The triangular-shaped interior is arranged over several different levels, each based around landmark sections of the aircraft. The tailplane protrudes from the façade, forming a dramatic entrance.

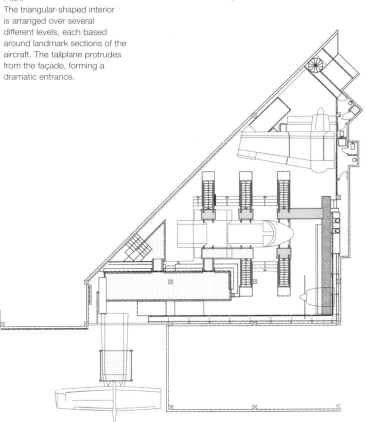

There may be plenty of aeroplanes with bars on board, but there can't be many bars that actually contain a plane the way the Caribou Hangar Bar, in Madrid, Spain, does. Architects Hector Ruiz-Velazquez and Javiar García García of Grupo Mat were asked to create a bar, discothèque and concert hall that resembled 'a typical American air force base bar, where the pilots finished with their duties would go to relax and hang out'. In response, Grupo Mat integrated the air force theme into their design concept by modelling the interior in the style of an aeroplane factory 'assembly line'. Authenticity was somewhat guaranteed by Grupo Mat purchasing an old 'Caribou' aircraft, which was then disassembled, with all the parts utilized to decorate and form the bar's interior.

Grupo Mat certainly know how to make an entrance. They have given Caribou a spectacular façade. The plain brick frontage of the former retail store, which has been clad in steel to appear like an aircraft hanger, supports the plane's tail, painted primary yellow with a blue back fin that sports the bar's name. Inside, the triangular-shaped space has been organized into multiple layers, arranged around landmark sections of the aircraft. Recycled stainless steel, iron and reclaimed wood have been used, along with the original plane parts, to create the industrial, warehouse-style interior. Strong coloured lighting adds warmth and serves to emphasize particular areas, such as chartreuse yellow on the main bar and reds and greens elsewhere.

Above:
The interior was modelled on an aeroplane factory assembly line. Hence the cross-section of the plane's fuselage displayed on the upper levels and the general suggestion of work in progress.

There are two bars – a long main bar, constructed from distressed timber, which overlooks the sunken dance floor to the centre of the space, and a second, smaller bar located beneath a suspended wing of the Caribou, close to the rear entrance. Mechanics' workbenches provided inspiration for the design of the main bar counter, which appears functional and suitably industrial, especially with the back-bar bottle display shelves that can be secured behind sliding metal cage doors. At one end of the bar, a propeller juts out like an elaborate metal fan. Bar stools, upholstered in aviator-style, 'Top Gun' brown leather, line the main bar, and surrounding the dance floor are communal seating benches, again fabricated from reclaimed and distressed materials.

Suspended above the dance floor is the main body of the aircraft, sliced in half to look like work in progress on the production line. Several staircases lead to upper platforms, which surround the hanging aeroplane. The bases of these stairways serve to define the borders of the dance area and the upper levels are furnished with more utilitarian bench seating to accommodate VIPs. Images from the 1940s, such as 'pin-up girls', were painted onto the walls to provide a final 'air force hanger' touch.

Absolut Icebar
Design: Arne Bergh and Åke Larsson
Sponsorship: Absolut Vodka

Antidote
Planning and design: CPM (Asia) Limited, Lead Designers:
John James Law and Simon Chim Pak Kee
Fitting-out contractor: Wing Kai Engineering Company Ltd.

Astro
Designer: Michael Young
Collaborators: Katrin Peturs, Jokull

B 018
Architect: Bernard Khoury
Client: B.A.4
Contractor: Ayoub
Structural engineering: Nadim Honein

Bar Lounge 808
Design project team: Plajer & Franz Studio – Werner Franz,
Christoph Hildebrand, Olaf Koeppen, Alexander Plajer
Lighting design: Plajer & Franz Studio
Shopfitter: Werkstätte für Innenausbau Berndt
Lighting fixtures: Fa. Neon Müller
Upholstery: Fa. Fronhöfer

BAR Ballad BAR
Client: Ballad Co., Ltd.
Interior designer: Glamorous Co., Ltd. (formerly Morita
Yasumichi Design Office)
Graphic design: Hiromura Masaaki of Hiromura Design Office
Lighting design: Ito Kenji of Maxray Inc.
Contractor: Nomura Co., Ltd.
In-house project team: Glamorous Co., Ltd. – Morita
Yasumichi, Sakagami Seiji; Kondo Yasuo Design Office –
Kondo Yasuo, Sakoh Katsuyuki; Super Potato Co., Ltd. –
Sugimoto Takashi, Wakabayashi Takae

Bar Lodi
Client: Sig. Corsano
Architect: Fabio Novembre
Design team: Marco Braga, Lorenzo de Nicola, Serena Novembre
General contractor: Gualina and Gualtieri

Bar Nil
Client: Luca Pavoni
Architects and lighting design: Lazzarini Pickering Architetti
Collaborator: Giuseppe Postet
Carpentry: Faiegnameria Orsini
Chairs: Harry Bertoia

Bar Tempo
Art direction: Shigeru Uchida
Architectural design: Aldo Rossi, Morris Adjmi, Toyota Horiguchi +
SDA

Interior and furniture design: Shigeru Uchida, Yoshimi Tanaka +
Studio 80
Graphic design: Katsumi Asaba
Producer: Mitsuhiro Kuzuwa + Jasmac
Owner: Kitakyushu City, Mojiko Development
Corporation Builder: FUJITA – Wakachiku Joint Enterprise in
Construction

Brown
Designer: Nu Nu Luan
Contractor: KCA & Associates
Lighting consultant: Juan Contin of CDG International
Restaurant management: Smooth Limited

Café L'Atlantique
Client: Ivano Fatibene
Architect: Fabio Novembre
General contractor: Sin

Caribou Hangar Bar
Design and construction: Grupo Mat

Chinawhite
Client: Rory Keegan and John Stephen
Interior designer: Cara Satmoko of Satmoko Ball Architecture
Interiors Architect: Munkenbeck & Marshall
Decorator: Melanie Fisher
Branding: Edward Ashley-Carter

Claridge's Bar
All fittings and furniture: David Collins
All items 'procured' by: Savoy Group

Crowne Plaza Bar
Architect: Adam D. Tihany International
Furniture: Colber srl
Decorative lighting: Sirmos
Fabric: Pollack; Corragio
Rugs: M & M design International
Logs/Feature table: Showman Fabricator

Dietrich's
Client: Daimler-Benz AG & Co, 'Fidelis'
Architect (of hotel): Rafael Moneo
Engineering and construction: Debis Immobilienmanagement
GmbH; IGH – Ingenieurgesellschaft; Drees &
Sommer/Kohlbecker Gesamtplan; 9-D design; Kep Servotel
Handelsgesellschaft

Disco
Architect: Isay Weinfeld
Collaboration: Domingos Pascali
Project team: Fausto Natsui, Isis Chaulon, Paulo Filisetti
Construction: Fairbanks e Pilnik
Dancefloor lighting: Ira Levy
Graphic design: Giovanni Bianco
Artistic panels: Humberto e Fernando Campana

Embassy
Architect: McconnellRayner
Bars: 'Solid surface material' by Marblo Pty Ltd
Booth screens: Futurtech Pty Ltd
Lighting design: Harron Robson Pty Ltd
Dining table pendant fittings: Designed by McconnellRayner;
manufactured by Planet Furniture

Float
Client: Giuseppe Burgio and Jeffrey Beers
Interior designer: Jeffrey Beers International (Project Team –
Jae Lee, Alan Shamoun, Julia Roth, Jill Stiely)
General contractor: Aries Construction
Lighting supplier: SLD Lighting
Lounge seating, banquettes, tables: Wood, Spring and Down

Hotel Atoll Bar
Client: Arne Weber
Architects: Alison Brooks Architects
Interior contractors: Framcke & Sohn Buchholz
Graphic designers: Mayer & Partner
Lighting designers: Peter Andres
Computer imaging: Softroom

Hudson Hotel Bar
Client: Ian Schrager Hotels
Design: Philippe Starck, Anda Andrei
Starck Design Studio: Bruno Borrione, Daniel Pouzet
Lighting design: Johnson Schwinghammer; Clark Johnson
Production architect: Polshek Partnership Architects

Jazz Matazz
Client: Fresk S.L.
Architects: Lluís Jubert and Eugenia Santacana
Constructor: Inox Moble S.L.

Leshko's
Designers: David Schefer and Eve-Lynn Schoenstein –
David Schefer Design, LLC
Owners: Bob Pontarelli and Stephen Heighton
Contractor: Kinery Group
Chairs: Saarinen through Knoll
Banquettes: Munrod
Ceiling light fabrication: And Bob's Your Uncle…
Decorative lighting: Global Lighting, Luce Plan, Lost City Arts
Stone: Cultured Stone
Vinyl: Momentum
Decorative glass: Bendheim
Back bar: Lumisite
Panels: Wheatstraw board through Architectural Systems
Table tops: Formica laminate fabricated by Chairs & Stools

Lux
Architects and designers: Manuel Reis, Fernando Fernandes,
Jose Miranda, Margarida Grácio Nunes,
Fernando Sanchez Salvador
Lighting design: Paulo Graça e Luís Cruz

Man Ray
Architects: M.C.M. Design
Joiner: Sodifra
Iron manufacturer: Dutemple
Sculptor: Bruno Tanquerel
Painter: Eliane Franc

Mandarin Bar
Architect: Adam D. Tihany International
Furniture and decorative lighting: Colber s.r.l.
Millwork: Fidec Associats, S.A.
Sofa fabric: Larson

Mink
Concept and design: Wayne Finschi

Miramar Hotel Bar
Client: Osracom Touristic Establishments
Architect and interior designer: Michael Graves & Associates,
New Jersey USA
Associate architect: Rami El Dahan & Soheir Fahid Architects
Interior design coordinator: Ibrahim Nagi
Landscape architect: Hydroscapes Egypt
Structural consultant: Hamza Associates
Engineering consultant: Bakry Engineers

NASA
Designer/Concept: Johannes Torpe/Turbo2000künstkontrolle Ltd.
Graphic design: Per Madsen/Johannes Torpe
In-house team/Clients: M.Fabricius/J.Torpe/K.Thurmann/P. Lipski
Main contractor: Niels Herholdt
Construction suppliers: Ronne & Brorsen
Electronics: Electric Design Company

Next
Architect: Álvaro Leite Siza Vieira
Stability: G.O.P. – Gabinete de Organização de Projectos

Page
Client: WAT International Co., Ltd.
Interior design: Glamorous Co., Ltd. (formerly Morita Yasumichi
Design Office) & Kondo Yasuo Design Office
Lighting design: Ito Kenjo of Maxray Inc.
Contractor: WAT International Co., Ltd.
Book producer: Yasuoka Yoichi
In-house project team: Glamorous Co., Ltd. – Morita Yasumichi,
Sakagami Seiji & Kondo Yasuo Design Office – Kondo Yasuo,
Sakai Atsushi

Purple Bar
Owner: Ian Schrager London Limited
Overall design: Philippe Starck, Anda Andrei

Red Sea Star
Interior design: Ayala S. Serfaty
Project architect: Sefi Kiryati
Design production: Aqua Creations
Chairs: NIA Israel

rumjungle
Client: Jeffrey Chodorow and Circus Circus Development
Interior designer: Jeffrey Beers International
Architect: Klai-Juba Architects
General contractor: M.J. Dean Construction
Lighting consultant: Thomas Thompson
Millwork and 'Rain Chandeliers': Roger B. Phillips
Waterwall contractor: Recreation Development Corp.
Terrazzo/Onyx flooring: Corradini

Shu
Client: Molino s.r.l.
Architect: Fabio Novembre
Design team: Marco Braga, Lorenzo de Nicola
General contractor: Technobeton
Lighting: Studio Pollige
Graphics: Marco Braga

Soft
Architect: Airconditioned
Tables and stools: El Ultimo Grito
Chairs: Jam
Sofa: Inflate

Orbit Bar
Architects: Burley Katon Halliday
Structural engineer: Steigter Clarey & Partners
Builder: Accor Asia Pacific
Lighting: Design Coalition
Chairs: Eero Saarinen tulip chairs

The Bomb
Architects: Lief Design
Lighting: Liacel
Seating: Distinctive Design
Sound: Superfi Pro

The Corinthian
Client: G1 Group
Architect: United Designers, overseen by CEO Keith Hobbs
Contractors: In-house team

The Church Lounge
Owner: Hartz Mountain Industries, Leonard and Emanuel Stern
Designer: Bogdanow Partners Architects
Lighting: Focus Lighting
General contractor: R. C. Dolner

The Seagram Brasserie
Design team: Diller + Scofidio, Charles Renfro (project leader),

Deane Simpson
Structural engineer: Alan Burden, Structured Environment
Lighting design: Richard Shaver
Video collaborator: Ben Rubin, Ear Studio
Script for entry installation: Douglas Cooper
Curtain design: Mary Bright
Graphics: 2X4
Artwork casting: Z Corporation
Outcast installation assisted by Matthew Johnson

The Supperclub
Owner: De Mattos Tres b.v. Bert van der Leden
Architects: Concrete Architectural Associates
Design team: Gilian Schrofer, Rob Wagemans, Erik van Dillen

Time (Intergalactic) Beach Bar
Architects: Paul Daly Design Studio
Poured flooring and specialist wall finish: Lasar Europe Ltd
General lighting: Light Attack
Specialist lighting: Jeremy Lord

Tsuki-No-Ie
Client: Prids. Co., Ltd.
Design: Glamorous Co., Ltd.
Lighting design: Ito Kenji of Maxray Inc.
Contractor: IMD Co., Ltd.
In-house project team: Morita Yasumichi, Fujii Akihiro

Zeppelin
Concept: Ekaterina Cvetkova, Georgy Petrushin
Architect: Boris Krutik
Artist: Boris Aiba
Stylist: Valeriya Manohina

Zoom
Client: Joseph Maria Portas i Bernat
Designers and work directors: Xavier Pau i Corominas and Jordi
Pau i Corominas
Interior designer: Mariana Roviras i Sampere
General construction coordinator: Pau Disseny Associats

Picture credits

Frederic Alm (97); Daniel Aubry (102); Bettmann/Corbis (8–11); David Brittain (16 right); Simon Brown (20); Friedrich Busam/Architekturphoto (54–59); Earl Carter (112–113); Reggie Casagrande (172–175); Jose Ruiz de Cenzano (184–187); Niall Clutton/ARCAID; Courtesy Concrete Architectural Associates (136–139); Luisa Ferreira (164–165); Alberto Ferrero (32–37, 46–49, 178–181); Robert Fretwell (160–163); Courtesy G1 Group (2–5); Chris Gascoigne (118–121); Peter Grant (95); Courtesy Michael Graves (103 left); Francisco Guedes (140); Jorg Hempel (94); David M Joseph (38–39); Ben Kelly (14); Christoph Kircherer (106–109); Michael Kleinberg (122–123); Alexey Knyazev (166–169); Andrew Lamb (90–91); Rob Lawson (3, 5, 22–23, 84–85, 124–125); Ari Magg (154–159); Mary Evans Picture Library (7); Courtesy of Ministry of Sound (15); Mihail Moldoveanu (110–111); Michael Moran (68–71); Michael Mundy (114–117); Nacasa & Partners (28–31, 40–41, 80–83, 86–89); Courtesy Marc Newson Ltd (19); Becky Nunes (60–61); Peter Paige Photography (92–93); Tina Paul 1987 (13); Anne Francoise Pellissier (126–133); Courtesy Perspective Magazine, Hong Kong (42–45); Matteo Piazza (152–153); Emmanuel Piron (18, 148–151); Eugeni Pons (146–147, 176–177); Sharon Rees (24–27); Tuca Reines (170–171); Tomoaki Sato (76–79); Albi Serfaty (50–53); Courtesy Alvaro Leite Siza (141); Courtesy Philippe Starck; Jens Stoltze (182–183); Alexander van Berge/Taverne Agency, production Ulrika Lundgren (96); Morley von Sternberg (6–9); Morley von Sternberg/ARCAID (104–105); Paul Warchol (64–67); Adrian Wilson (90–91, 98–101, 134–135); Michael S Yamashita/Corbis (12); Leo Yu - Blue Hydrant (62–63); Hans Zeegers/Taverne Agency (103).

Drawing on page 6 by R & G Cruikshank, taken from Pierce Egan's *Life in London*.

The publisher has endeavoured to provide full and accurate credits for all projects and pictures featured in this book. If there are any mistakes or omissions, please contact us and we shall correct them in future editions.

Laurence King Publishing

Acknowledgements

I would like to thank all the architecture and design practices, bar owners, press officers and photographers who have spared their precious time and provided me with the inspiration, information and material that has made this book possible.

I am most grateful to Nick Barham, Roger Cave, Sudeep Gohil, Astrid Klein, Mark Leib and Sylvia Warren for their advice on which designer bars to investigate in their respective corners of the globe. Thanks also to Andy Bishop and *Mondo* magazine, and to Aidan Walker for proving that name-dropping can be productive.

At Laurence King Publishing, I would like to thank Commissioning Editor Jo Lightfoot, as well as Jennifer Hudson, Helen McFarland and Susan Lawson for their patience and persistence in researching and gathering all the information (occasionally from sources that were not quite on this planet), which made my work as painless as possible. To my editor Simon Cowell, whose advice, intelligence and humour have helped everything make sense and kept me sane, many thanks.

Designer Matt Baxter, it's been a 'Blast' – thanks for making things seem so easy even when they're not. To Robert Lawson, James Burgess, Mark Quinn and Lorraine Richer, thank you for the favours – I owe you one.

To all my friends, family and colleagues, especially the design team at CLASS, a tremendous thank you for putting up with the seemingly endless saga of 'the book'. I'm ready for that drink now.

And, finally, thank you to Joan Ryder and Angus Winchester for your love and support. This book is for you both.